Career Development
of the
Effective College Teacher

Price $1.00

The Project to Improve College Teaching

jointly sponsored by the American
Association of University Professors and
the Association of American Colleges
and supported by a grant from
the Carnegie Corporation
from September 1969 to 1971.

Advisory Board

Additional copies of CAREER DEVELOPMENT OF THE EFFEC-
TIVE COLLEGE TEACHER are available from the American Association of University Professors, One Dupont Circle, Washington, D.C.
20036, at $1.00 per copy. Also, THE RECOGNITION AND EVALU-
ATION OF TEACHING is still available for $1.00 per copy.

First printing, November 1971

II

career development of the effective college teacher

BY KENNETH E. EBLE
AND THE CONFERENCE ON
CAREER DEVELOPMENT

SPONSORED BY THE A.A.C.
AND THE A.A.U.P.

CONTENTS

Preface

PARTICIPANTS IN CONFERENCES ON CAREER DEVELOPMENT

sponsored by

The Project to Improve College Teaching

San Francisco, May 7 and 8, 1971

Clinton Adams, Dean, Fine Arts, University of New Mexico

Ronald Bauer, Assistant Professor, Electrical Engineering, University of California at Los Angeles

Chester Case, Director, Cooperative Internship Program, University of California at Berkeley

Ruth Eckert, Professor, Higher Education, University of Minnesota

Jerry G. Gaff, Assistant Research Psychologist, Center for Research and Development in Higher Education, University of California at Berkeley

Edward A. Hay, Geology, De Anza College

Robert E. Helbling, Chairman, Foreign Languages, University of Utah

Sam Kelly, Director, Center for Higher Education, Western Washington State College

Marsha Kinder, Assistant Professor, English, Occidental College

Walter D. Knight, Dean, Letters and Science, University of California at Berkeley

Lee Anne Miller, Assistant Professor, Fine Arts, University of Missouri at Kansas City

Richard H. Peairs, Director, Western Regional Office, American Association of University Professors

Burton E. Sabol, Assistant Professor, English, University of Oregon

L. Shelbert Smith, Director, Ford Foundation Project for Developing Institutions, American Association of University Professors

Cornelius Steelink, Professor, Chemistry, University of Arizona

Donald W. Treadgold, Professor, History, University of Washington

Virginia Voeks, Professor, Psychology, San Diego State College

Franklin Wallin, Provost and Dean of Faculty, Colgate University

Gregory B. Wolfe, President, Portland State University

Washington, D.C., May 8 and 9, 1970

Leonard Archer, Professor, English and Speech, Tennessee A&I State University

Conrad Balliet, Associate Professor, English, Wittenberg University

Mark Beach, Associate Dean, College of Arts and Sciences, University of Rochester

Edward J. Bloustein, President, Bennington College

W. Donald Bowles, Vice President for Academic Affairs, American University

Beryl Brown, Graduate Student, Psychology, University of Michigan

Ruth Eckert, Professor, Higher Education, University of Minnesota

Edward D. Eddy, President, Chatham College

Peter Elbow, Associate Professor, Humanities, Massachusetts Institute of Technology

Frank W. Finger, Professor, Psychology, University of Virginia

Dorothy Goodwin, Assistant Provost, University of Connecticut

Judith Hakola, Assistant Dean, Arts and Sciences, University of Maine

Robert E. Helbling, Chairman, Foreign Languages, University of Utah

Linda B. Kahan, Assistant Professor, Biology, Antioch College

Maynard Mack, Professor, English, Yale University

H. C. McBay, Professor, Chemistry, Morehouse College

Wilbert McKeachie, Chairman, Psychology, University of Michigan

Neill Megaw, Chairman, English, University of Texas

Kiyo Morimoto, Bureau of Study Council, Harvard University

Patricia R. Plante, Associate Professor, English, Towson State College

Galen Pletcher, Faculty of Philosophical Studies, Southern Illinois University

Jacquelyn Mattfeld, Dean, Sarah Lawrence College

Eugene Runyon, Chairman, Psychology, Central State University

W. Hugh Stickler, Chairman, Education, Florida State University

Jim Sutton, Graduate Student, Higher Education, University of Iowa

Robert Van Waes, Associate Secretary, American Association of University Professors

Franklin Wallin, Provost and Dean of Faculty, Colgate University

W. Max Wise, Professor, Higher Education, Columbia Teachers College

Atlanta, May 19, 1970

L. Shelbert Smith, Director, Ford Foundation Project for Developing Institutions, American Association of University Professors

Leonard Archer, English, Tennessee A&I State University

Joseph Bennett, History, North Carolina A&T University

George Breathett, Social Studies, Bennett College

Jean Bright, English, North Carolina A&T University

Robert Brisbane, Political Science, Morehouse College

W. M. Clark, Biology, Bishop College

Evelyn Garrity, Chemistry, Jackson State College

Hugh M. Gloster, President, Morehouse College

Faye Goldberg, Psychology, Morehouse College

Ralph Martin, Education, Knoxville College

James Mayo, Physics, Morehouse College

William McArthur, Biology, Knoxville College

Rogers Newman, Mathematics, Southern University (Baton Rouge)

Gertrude Ridgel, Biology, Kentucky State College

Eugene Runyon, Psychology, Central State University

Alberta Seaton, Biology, Texas Southern University

Julius Taylor, Physics, Morgan State College

Charles Temple, Alabama A&M College

Daniel Thompson, Sociology, Dillard University

Prince Wilson, Executive Director, Atlanta University Center Corporation

Aurelia Young, Music, Jackson State College

Career Development
of the Effective
College Teacher

Introduction

Like the project's earlier booklet, *The Recognition and Evaluation of Teaching,* this one is a collaborative effort. The conference participants listed on the preceding pages were vital to defining the subject and to furnishing much of the substance. Between the date of the first conference, May 8 and 9, 1970, and the second, May 7 and 8, 1971, the director spent a large part of his time exploring various aspects of career development.

Chiefly, this involved gathering and studying information and visiting some seventy colleges and universities talking with students, faculty, and administrators. In addition, the project made an informal national survey, through the first Career Development Report, of systematic efforts being made to further the career development of effective teachers. The results of that survey were almost totally negative. Only six of some 150 respondents identified their institutions as having effective faculty development systems, and three of those identified were outside the continental United States: University of British Columbia, University of Puerto Rico, and University of Hawaii.

This survey, it should be stated, gives an imperfect indication of the presence or absence of career development systems. The questionnaire was brief and went out as part of an insert in *Academe,* the AAUP newsletter. The respondents were all members of faculties, and they may not accurately reflect the existence of opportunities for career development. The questionnaire was tucked away on the back page of the report, and the percentage of response was very small.

Nevertheless, the overwhelmingly negative response probably does speak to a general absence of effective career development programs in higher education. None of my talks at individual colleges (where I was able to ask detailed and specific questions) revealed conditions at much variance with those reported in the survey. And in both conferences, the 50 or so participants representing a variety of faculty and administrators also supported the conclusions that colleges and universities do very little to develop their personnel as teachers.

The project's initial hope was to locate effective systems for career development and to make them known to the profession at large. The dearth of systematic efforts has somewhat altered the design of the booklet. Though we have introduced throughout the test examples of useful practices at one institution and another, we have not attempted to describe at length any one institution's total but often scattered efforts. Instead, we have attempted to discuss the problems and possibilities of career development as they may appear in relation to individual needs and aspirations at various stages in a career and to characteristics and aims of colleges and universities.

Chapter Seven deals with special problems of the community colleges, the predominantly Negro colleges, and the careers of academic women. Obviously, the project could only touch upon these important concerns, but not to discuss them at all would have been a graver omission. In respect to the Negro colleges, the project was able to sponsor a joint conference with another AAUP project, a Ford Foundation supported program for assistance to developing institutions, in Atlanta, May 19, 1970. Participants in that conference are also listed in the preceding pages.

The project is indebted to all the conference participants and to the many individuals who, through correspondence and conversation, contributed to the substance of the booklet. The members of the San Francisco conference gave final shape and substance to the outline. They also read the final draft, and its present form owes much to their careful scrutiny and suggestions. Fortunately, that group included an artist, Lee Anne Miller, who contributed the cover design.

The Project to Improve College Teaching completed its two years of activities under a grant from the Carnegie Corporation in September 1971. The sponsoring associations, the Association of American Colleges and the American Association of University Professors, will continue to make project materials available. Through their own committees, the two associations will continue to work in directions the project has helped to define.

Kenneth E. Eble
November, 1971

1. Aspects of Career Development

Even the phrase "career development" is not right. Too pretentious, on the one hand, as is much of the academic tradition, and too mundane, as if careers, like alumni-giving, might respond positively to development efforts. Yet, the subject is much on the minds of those in academic careers and prominent in the current concern for teaching, teaching load, tenure, and accountability.

The phrase, then, might be regarded as a necessary shorthand. The subject itself can be defined chronologically beginning with early identification of potentially gifted teachers and their development as teachers and scholars in the graduate school. The next logical step is to consider what happens to the teacher within the college or colleges where he or she achieves professorial rank and tenure. Finally the concern with growth and development through periods of apprenticeship and achieved competence moves on to questions of teaching commitment, competence, vigor as professors move toward retirement.

Some of the Problems

There is no ideal professor and probably few in the profession move through the sequence of development just as it is described in these chapters. A recognition of this diversity came out in the San Francisco conference where the discussion, despite its chronological format, seemed to focus naturally upon such themes as *the reward system, flexibility, leadership,* and *forces for change.* In the earlier conference, the groups identified the following as most important to improving career development opportunities for undergraduate teachers:

1. The need to improve the preparation of teachers in the graduate school.

1

2. The establishment of adequate career development systems as part of regular institutional policies and practices.

3. Leadership from deans, department chairmen, and other administrators and faculty in supporting and encouraging teaching excellence.

4. Bettering the lot of teaching assistants.

5. Examining the myths and stereotypes which adversely affect teaching and teachers. For example, that tenure is to blame for poor teaching, that research is incompatible with teaching, that there is some one truly effective teaching style, that small classes are always better than large, and the like.

6. Fostering the exchange in teaching assignments among faculty members in different colleges and universities and within a single institution.

7. Increasing opportunities for teachers who may wish or need to seek a temporary or permanent change from a teaching career.

In addition, that conference group placed emphasis upon learning more about the teaching-learning process itself. Specifically it called for:

1. Increased emphasis upon recognizing and rewarding effective teaching.

2. Increased opportunities for professors to observe other teaching styles and to develop effective styles of their own.

3. Examination of whether current student attitudes and expectations have diminished the effectiveness of traditional ways of teaching.

This does not include all the topics discussed at the two conferences, but it does emphasize the recurring topics and provides a way of looking at the whole subject before giving specific attention to the possible stages of development in an individual teacher's career.

Both conferences and discussions during my campus visits came to the same general conclusion: except for support of research, institutions and the profession do little to develop college faculty members as teachers. Within institutions, the setting aside of a specific percentage of a budget for faculty development is a very uncommon practice. Within the profession at large, the forces which work against undergraduate teaching are probably as great as those which work for it.

Results of the Questionnaire

The response to the Career Development questionnaire sent out by the Project offers some substantiation of the general deficiency. Faculty members from 142 different institutions were overwhelmingly negative in response to the main question: *My institution (does, does not) have an effective faculty development system.* A study, *Faculty Development Procedures in Small Colleges/A Southern Survey,* (SREB 1963), by W. Starr Miller and Kenneth M. Wilson, reached similar conclusions:

> While there are activities in these colleges directed toward establishing or improving approaches to faculty development, these activities are, in the main, uncoordinated and lacking in creativity . . . . There is extensive use of certain procedures, yes. But often reliance is placed on a limited number of relatively routine procedures and emphasis tends to be placed on procedures related to the process of orienting faculty members to the institution — an important but limited aspect of the process of development.

In response to the second question: *Outside of the departmental program and budget, my institution provides specific support for (research, teaching, service),* about 60 percent of the respondents reported specific support for research. About ten percent reported specific support for teaching, and even fewer for service. Eighteen respondents said their institutions offered *no support* outside of department budgets for research, teaching, or service. Those few replies which identified effective faculty development systems indicated that institutional support was provided for all three.

The third question was aimed at the most common form of institutional support for faculty development or renewal, the sabbatical leave. Some form of sabbatical was reported at about 60 percent of the institutions. Replies from a number of prominent universities, however, University of North Carolina, Wisconsin, Iowa, Rutgers, Purdue, Vanderbilt, Pittsburgh, and Texas, indicated that sabbatical leaves either did not exist or were of such a nature as to be disregarded by the faculty respondent.

Awarding of sabbatical leaves at about one-fourth of the schools depended upon specific research proposals. Somewhat fewer reported that a plan for improving one's teaching, a research proposal, a proposal for general professional development were all acceptable as adequate justification for granting a sabbatical.

The question on sabbaticals provoked a good deal of voluntary criticism penciled in on the returns. Respondents were irritated by the restrictions placed upon the granting of sabbatical leaves and suspicious of the way in which those who received leaves were chosen.

The last two questions on the survey were aimed at discovering the presence or absence of specific preparation for college teaching in the graduate programs. Over half of this group responded negatively to the question: *Aside from departmental course work, my department's graduate program (includes, does not include) specific preparation for college teaching.* The final question asked for details of the specific preparation for college teaching which might be going on in a graduate program. The possibilities listed on the questionnaire were: *classes in education, expertly supervised teaching experience, use of audio or video tape, departmental seminars or classes in teaching, other.* Though all of these were reported at one school or another, no respondent indicated the presence of a comprehensive program.

Other Studies

Some additional information in respect to preparation in the graduate schools is obtainable from a number of sources. Donald Dean's booklet, *Preservice Preparation of College Biology Teachers: A Search for a Better Way,* is one recent source. It brings together the investigation and conferences held by CUEBS, The Commission on Undergraduate Education in the Biological Sciences, to confront the problem within that discipline. A CUEBS study of 94 leading universities awarding 1843 Ph.D. degrees in biological fields in 1963-67, showed that 66 percent provided no special training to teaching assistants before they taught and 80 percent offered no special course or seminar in any aspect of college teaching. This lack of attention, on the one hand, and a strong feeling for remedying that lack, on the other, were prominent in all of CUEBS' regional and national conferences. A survey of graduate schools granting the majority of Ph.D. degrees in English reveals much the same condition.

Ann Heiss's book, *Challenges to Graduate Schools,* (Jossey-Bass, 1970), closely examines Ph.D. programs at ten graduate schools and reports on various other comprehensive surveys. A review of graduate programs in 450 institutions in 1967 indicated that in 75 percent of these, the teaching assistantship was the primary means for preparing future college teachers. And though 95 percent of these institutions described the assistantship as an opportunity for teaching under supervision and guidance, other studies suggest that fewer than half of those who held such appointments were likely to receive adequate, systematic, or continuous guidance from a senior member of the faculty. Few programs designed to prepare graduates for college teaching are interdisciplinary, and few graduate students take course work in any aspect of teaching or learning.

What the project's modest and imperfect questionnaire reveals, then, is supported by other studies, other conferences, and by faculty members, administrators, and graduate students at individual colleges and universities. Indeed, the administrators at the two PICT conferences were as outspoken as faculty in pointing out the present deficiencies. Clearly, all evidence points to the fact that neither individual institutions nor the profession itself give sufficient attention to faculty development.

Dimensions of the Problem: The Reward System

Everywhere I have gone in the past two years, members of the academic community single out the reward system as the crucial factor in improving undergraduate teaching. The initial arguments tend to be more negative than positive. At the simplest, they are attacks on publish or perish, or complaints about the difficulties professors face if they wish to give themselves largely to under-graduate teaching. As discussion develops, wider dimensions of the problem appear. I think the following generalizations fairly describe the situation:

1. Graduate work with its heavy emphasis upon specialized scholarly study within the disciplines and with large amounts of support from outside the university has dominated the development of faculty and institutions in the past 20 years.

2. The individual entering the profession is shaped by the values held by the graduate school and enforced by the individual institution and the profession at large.

3. These values hold that the highest level of achievement for the college professor as teacher is the development of specialized students within the discipline at the most advanced level of study. These values place great emphasis upon continuing scholarly accom-plishments and assume that a highly qualified professor will devote half of his time or more to research.

These generalizations are stated in a plain and unelaborated way, for arguments involving the values of individual professors are shot through with specific and heated arguments that obscure the value basis from which they proceed. The generalizations are also more applicable to the large universities and prestigious colleges. But even in those many small colleges where teaching is clearly primary, faculty members feel the effects of the values held by the graduate schools from which they came, by the disciplines to which they belong, and by those institutions which tend to set the style and standards for all higher education.

The uneven development of higher education stands out sharply in the recent but probably continuing surplus of Ph.D. degrees in almost all disciplines. It is to be found more complexly involved in the growth of the community colleges which has been a phenomenon of the past decade. Because of the pressures of the market, graduate departments are now taking an interest in the community college, a whole sector of higher education which they had previously ignored.

The accomplishments of the graduate school need not be called into question here. It is enough to note such facts as the disparity between the needs of the four-year and community colleges and the production of Ph.D.'s in the graduate school, the favorable conditions which outside funding and institutional support provided for the development of graduate work, and the present changes in support, attitudes, and needs which affect higher education at all levels. All of these have tended to call the operating principles of the reward system into question. At the same time, the questions themselves indicate how slowly the reward system responds to the need for change.

Publish or Perish

Much of what could be said about the reward system is caught up in the endless controversy over "publish or perish." The issue has been worked over in American higher education as intensely and for as long a period as any issue. Perhaps it is one of those important questions about education, such as freedom vs. discipline, specialization vs. generalization, the elective vs. the required curriculum, which are not to be solved but to be examined. In that continuing examination, we may define our principles and shape our practices.

A review of the debate over publish or perish is not possible here. Rather, the intent is to look at some of the arguments as they relate to the problems of advancing the career of the effective college teacher.

It is probably true, for example, that at some institutions "an excessive attention to teaching by a young professor may be assurance that he will soon be teaching somewhere else." It is also probably true that many institutions exert no great pressure on faculty members to publish or even to continue research. But it is unlikely that a profession which uses the term *higher education,* that defines personnel by academic rank, that has as its route of admission an advanced degree granted in large part by a small number of institutions, can escape from using visible scholarly achievements as a chief measure of an individual's worth. I am not arguing that this should or should not be. I am merely stating that something like "publishing," making known one's qualities of mind to those one has reason to respect, will have considerable influence on a professor's aspiration, practices, and frustrations. I doubt very much that the influence can be altogether avoided.

The questions raised by "publish or perish" cannot be shrugged aside. Teaching and research are both compatible and incompatible. It seems reasonable to insist that most of college teaching be informed by continuing scholarship or practice. That this insistence should take the form of published research seems dubious. The largest amounts of teaching are to the general student at introductory levels, and it is here that the distance is greatest between teaching and research which may result in publication. Nevertheless, there appears to me to be some harm in arguing that research is altogether incompatible with teaching and surely great harm in thinking that if one were released from scholarly obligations, good teaching would follow.

At the same time, it is obvious that for much of teaching in many disciplines, research and teaching are competing activities. One cannot write a book and talk about it at the same time. One cannot be doing painstaking laboratory work and demonstrating basic principles to a roomful of students at the same time. These are physical facts, not questions of value. Were we able to conduct our lives within one seamless garment we might move from one place to another with little disturbance of our basic posture at all times as learner, teacher, searcher, researcher, and creator. But until great numbers of the professoriate are able to function in this way, the profession will continue to feel the effects of "publish or perish."

As matters stand, advanced degree programs, the presence of departments and disciplinary associations, and the tangibility of published scholarly work, all operate to give this aspect of a professor's work higher visibility than any other. Second, the emphasis upon graduate work as a means of building an institution has created a market condition where the published scholar is in demand. Third, an impressive industry has grown up around scholarship, from book publishing to the manufacturers of equipment to the hotel and transportation and liquor industries dependent upon conventioneering.

Very little exists to shift the reward system in favor of teaching. It is not idle talk (though justifiably irritating to many faculty members) to say that teaching is its own reward. In various job satisfaction studies, faculty members indicate that the relationship with students is a major source of satisfaction. And it can also be argued that faculty members who derive great satisfaction from working with students, devote their energies to it, and make an impact upon students, do receive local recognition. Through a handful of teaching awards given by professional disciplines and the Harbison Distinguished Teaching Award program of the Danforth foundation, they may even achieve national recognition.

But we must search to find many forces working toward rewarding the teacher. And some of the forces that seem to favor teaching may turn out to work against it. The more successful one is as a teacher, the more students he gets to teach; the more he demands in the teaching-learning processes, the more attendant work he has to do: counseling, testing and grading, writing recommendations, serving on committees. In short, successful teaching may not only be somewhat outside the conventional reward system; it may stand in the way of pursuing those activities which would fit the system. There appears to be good reason for the claims that the development of effective college teachers resides in the creation of a reward system favorable to teaching. A later chapter will discuss the reward system at length.

Flexibility

In the discussions of career development, the need for *flexibility* comes up again and again. Flexibility within the reward system, for example, would not only provide more incentives to the teacher but more adequate support for other aspects of professional development. From one point of view, the chief fault with the reward system is that it seems to limit the ways in which one can gain both prestige and material rewards. And when the system is modified to include other aspects of a professor's work, it seems to propose that every professor embrace all virtues. Asked to perform as a great scholar, brilliant teacher, academic statesman, counselor to youth, and contributor to public good, the average professor may respond by being average in all respects.

Yet we know that human talents and human inclinations do not exist uniformly within either an individual or a profession. The need within the reward system may be to expect less in the way of total competence and more in the way of developing that which the person can do best, wants to do best. With such a reward system, a larger number of professors might be able to give first priority to teaching for longer periods of time.

By increasing the flexibility of practices and structures, a college might be able to make the most of the diverse talents and inclinations of faculty members and in some relation to the individual development of each. Respecting different kinds of teaching, providing opportunities for such variety, enabling teachers to move in and out of various teaching assignments, widening the opportunities for experiences in other institutions or in other careers, opening up alternatives when teachers grow stale or find certain directions blocked — these are examples of kinds of flexibility which appear beneficial to teachers.

Leadership

None of these can work to best advantage unless the administrative structures and administrators within them support such measures. There is widespread criticism of sabbatical leaves, for example, because they do not offer in practice what they seem to promise in the college handbook. The fault, setting aside the tendency to blame everything on a lack of funds, is the failure of institutions and of individuals having positions of power within them either to recognize the importance of such measures or to push for their effective operation.

Throughout the discussions of the last two years, the lack of effective leadership was constantly referred to. No one can say that the college and university are not sufficiently structured. But structure is not enough. The difference between a good department chairman and a poor one is probably seen most in relation to career development. For it is through the chairman that the reward system affects the individual faculty member. It is through the chairman that the institutional structures, the reward system itself, can be treated flexibly. Attitudes vary widely as to what a chairman should be. He may be caretaker, functionary, prestige figure, sacrificial victim. But where he affects any sizable number of individual faculty members — five or six should be enough to cause concern — he must be a leader, in old-fashioned terms, a shaper and molder of persons. He has a wide choice, I think in the ways of going about it — by quiet example, by restless assertion, by boldness and even bluster — but he must be capable of assessing the strengths and weaknesses, the desires and frustrations, the dispositions and commitments of his faculty if career development is to prosper at the most basic level.

In a small college, a dean probably plays a role similar to that of a chairman. In large colleges, the dean may be chiefly a center of distribution and control. In my experience of the past two years, deans have not emerged as leaders in effective and active support of teaching. There are exceptions, of course, but even these seem to consist of men who have risen above the nature of the office.

In the large institutions, teaching, if it is given specific attention by the dean's office, is often assigned to an associate or assistant dean. Such an assignment may carry with it the lessened importance attached to most institutional sub-functions. In recent years, the creation of the specific office of "dean of undergraduate instruction" has begun to appear. If such deans have prestige and power equal to that of college deans or the dean of the graduate school, they should be able to provide the effective attention to undergraduate teaching which I find missing in the present administrative structure.

As it is, deans could have much impact upon the career development of effective college teachers. They have, in most colleges, power of review and recommendation in matters of retention, promotion, and tenure. They have a good deal to do with the allocation of money within the college. They have some power to initiate programs independent of or in cooperation with departmental structures. Perhaps the dean's office has too much to do with the ordinary operations of the college to focus effective and continuing attention upon faculty development. Operating at some remove from the actualities of the classroom, a dean may not give the improvement of teaching a high priority.

These remarks are directed more to the position of dean than to the men who may occupy those positions. I think that position is a part of the conventional administrative pattern that might well be examined with a view to making it a more consequential force for improving instructional policies and practices.

In my travels, academic vice-presidents have been more visible than deans. They seem often to be men of strong interest in the instructional program. They also, I think, recognize the imbalances that exist between science and the humanities, the graduate school and the undergraduate program, the lower division and the upper division. Deans tend to see these imbalances somewhat as department chairmen see them: in terms of a department's or college's own best interest. Academic vice-presidents seem to see larger and appear to have both more freedom and more power to affect change. Men like Frank Wallin at Colgate, Paul Saltman at UC San Diego, Frank Vattano at Colorado State, to mention a few of the many I have met, are not afraid to push their ideas, to think larger than the limitations on budget, and to use their power. Many of the improvements of teaching within individual schools have been put in motion by the academic vice-president or someone in that office.

Although the project's work has not put me in touch with a great many presidents, I think that only in the small colleges do presidents have much to do with the development of teachers or the improvement of teaching. Perhaps my favorable impressions of academic vice-presidents suggests that presidents are delegating authority successfully. But presidents can be important and, by default, have been important in the decline of undergraduate teaching. Universities, even colleges in the past ten years, have not been built by placing emphasis there, and presidents have not often attempted to push in that direction. Given the encouragement that a renewed public interest in undergraduate education may provide, presidents may be important forces in the improvement of college teaching in the seventies.

Harold Dodd's *The Academic President — Educator or Caretaker?* (McGraw-Hill, 1962), proposes that because "the need for educational statesmanship is so compelling," a president should carve out 50 percent of his time for education. "The fulfillment of a president's purpose for his college or university," he writes, "is less a matter of esoteric philosophy than the embodiment of generalized aims in a series of specific, achievable goals. No one can match the president as potentially the most effective person to guide the thinking of both faculty and trustees toward higher degrees of specificity and clarity."

Some faculty members on every faculty become possessors of power which might be usefully employed in behalf of teaching, but in the big universities, they seldom exert force beyond a given department. In the smaller schools, the charismatic faculty member creates both support and antagonism. In all schools the power that might be exercised by the individual faculty member is characteristically diminished by containing him within committees. Insofar as higher educational institutions have played the game of competing for the eminent, nationally-recognized scholar, faculty power, in an individual sense, does not particularly support teaching, nor does it do much to foster the growth of the teaching professor.

Faculty senates have within their power the ability to do a good deal for teaching. Here and there, they have exercised such power, for example, in committees for teaching under one name or another at the University of California at Davis, the University of Toledo, the University of Delaware. At the University of Washington, the Faculty Senate was the body which moved the faculty to expand the use of student evaluation. Still, for the most part faculty senates are entangled in university business which keeps all members at a distance from such a thing as teaching itself. Members of such bodies, students and faculty alike, are probably doomed to go on protesting against all the trivia which consumes their time and longing for a confrontation with the big issues — like what should be spent on what — or the tangible ones — like classroom teaching.

Despite the prevailing bureaucracy in higher education, there are still centers of power within individual colleges and universities. It is still possible for individuals, offices, and committees to exercise power on behalf of teaching. Only in the very big universities have I observed a general and dispiriting stagnation, which may be both cause and effect of student unrest. Even there, within some departments, some larger units, a sense of being able to affect teaching for the good still remains. If faculty development is to achieve effective mechanisms within the structure, someone in a position of power must take the lead.

Forces for Change

This entire discussion stresses a need for change, to some degree a change from a quality control model to a developmental one. It is of considerable interest that the evaluation of teaching has been the most visible part of the project's work. Although evaluation has come about largely through the students, support of evaluation comes from both faculty and administration, as well. There are many reasons that evaluation gains attention. What I wish to stress here is the relation of evaluation to systems of career development.

Clearly an interest in evaluation, pushed by students, supported by administrations, and accepted by faculties is one of the forces moving toward support of career development. If there are ways of evaluating teaching, then there must be ways of developing effectiveness in teaching. In political terms, if a faculty is to take on greater responsibility in evaluating teaching, then it is likely to ask that the administration give greater support to the development of teachers. If, as a result, more attention were to be placed on faculty development, then surely some of what was being learned about teaching would go into developing faculty personnel.

The agitation against tenure and with it, collective bargaining, may alter attitudes to career development. Though tenure is attacked because it forces a life-long association between tenured faculty members and the institution, that fact has not seemed to give high priority to efforts to make the most of faculty personnel. Though a probationary period is a feature of tenure, little is actually done within that period to assist the young faculty member in developing his competence. The weakening of tenure would be likely to weaken already inadequate career development efforts. Nor do I think that collective bargaining in its initial stages will place faculty development ahead of such basic issues as salary, working conditions, fringe benefits, and the like. Finally, the uniform salary schedule frequently supported in the community colleges also leaves little room for an effective career development system.

The point of these remarks is that some forces for change are working toward giving consequential attention to faculty development. In addition, more general currents of change may make the profession more hospitable to the scholar who wishes to give his greatest commitment to teaching. I think public attention upon undergraduate teaching may force institutions to shift some of the emphasis away from graduate research. And I think it is a fair bet that the reforms which have been picking away at points of irritation within the old system — grades, credits and class hours, modes of instruction, calendar, housing and learning arrangements, and the like — may give way to larger reforms. These include changing attitudes toward open admissions, shortening the time for and widening the ways of getting the undergraduate degree, and breaking down the barriers between the college and the outside world. In many respects, these reforms threaten the college teacher's traditional professorial role. But in most respects, it seems to me, they diversify the opportunities and attractions of a college teaching career and may even increase the rewards for a commitment to teaching.

2. Preparing College Teachers

The Report of the AAUP Committee on College and University Teaching, investigating the improvement of college teaching 40 years ago, placed heavy emphasis upon attracting superior personnel to the profession. Its recommendations were aimed both at encouraging more of those "who combine scholarly competence of a high order with an inspiring personality," and discouraging those "of undistinguished ability and indifferent personal traits who are diligently grubbing their way to the doctorate." "All this," this section of the report concluded, "is especially to be desired during the next few years when the number of applicants for teaching positions in American universities and colleges is likely to be far in excess of the number of vacancies."

Reading the earlier AAUP Report, one is inclined to feel that little has changed since then. The ills which were pointed out in the earlier report seemed to reassert themselves in the decades of affluence and growth just past. As in the thirties, those conditions seem to be coming to an end. Once again, the profession has the need to take stock, and crucial to that examination is the place of teaching. Not only do we need to seek the best ways of selecting out of an abundance of talent the potentially gifted teachers, but also the best ways of providing a graduate experience that will develop graduate students' teaching abilities and motivate them to become superior teachers as they go on in their careers.

Ruth Eckert, who has spent much of her career studying motivations and job satisfactions of faculty members, places great emphasis upon the need to identify prospective college teachers earlier and to give them encouragement from that moment on. In a paper prepared for the first Career Development conference, she writes:

. . . much more could be done to recruit highly able, imaginative students to careers in college teaching. Unless we want to fill college teaching posts in the years ahead with Ph.D.'s frustrated in their efforts to obtain graduate teaching or research appointments, individuals with genuine interest in teaching should be deliberately recruited during undergraduate years — and with special attention given to tapping the talent potential of women and other disadvantaged groups.

Going On to Graduate School

Any attempt to enhance careers for individuals who will become effective college teachers depends upon facing the practices and attitudes of the graduate school. For the decision to become a college teacher comes late, according to Eckert's and other's studies, and for many may not be a firm decision until after the individual has begun graduate work. An identification of potentially gifted college teachers scarcely exists in public school or collegiate institutions, though the general encouragement of "bright" students to continue on at ever higher levels of formal education is a crude identifying process. Unfortunately, such a process tends to select those in conformity with existing patterns and to weed out those who don't fit a rather narrow range of academic achievement.

The processes of admitting students to graduate work is not much more refined. If anything, the variety in applicants is further diminished by the strong emphasis placed on grades in a major or scores in the major field on the Graduate Record Examination. At the level of Ph.D. candidacy, letters of recommendation become more important but these, too, tend to reinforce the statistical information about academic achievements and strongly stress the ability to do research work. The general question of the student's potential as a teacher is seldom raised, and specific questions which might bear upon future competence in teaching — breadth as well as depth, a lively curiosity, a desire to work with students, an ability to synthesize and clarify, a command of verbal communication — are minor matters if they are asked at all.

Despite the absence of efforts to identify college teaching potential or to give importance to such potential in admitting students to Ph.D. work, graduate students seem to gain an awareness that teaching will be a large part of their future career. In a recent study of eleven graduate departments at Stanford, a high percentage of graduate students in the social sciences, humanities, and languages gave "becoming a college or university teacher" as a very important reason for undertaking graduate work. In only two of the science departments was "becoming a research worker" given by a larger percentage of students, though "acquiring scholarly competence in the discipline" was judged very important by a high percentage of students in departments in both science and mathematics and the social sciences.

By contrast, the percentage of these students rating the departmental graduate faculty "high" in "interest in student's development as a college teacher" ranged from 3 percent to 26 percent in seven departments in social science, humanities and languages. The Stanford survey (part of Ann Heiss's study of Ph.D. programs) clearly shows the prominence teaching has for graduate students in the Humanities and Languages as contrasted with those in Science and Mathematics and the Social Sciences. Research in the latter departments is clearly most important, and both students and faculty, as reflected in responses to the survey, seem clear about it. In the other departments, students seem to be less apprised of departmental aims and less in tune with the faculty's values. Such differences within the university must be kept in mind in the general discussion of graduate work.

Because graduate schools are fewer and higher than other institutions, the passage from graduate school to teaching position is almost always down. Attitudes developed in the graduate school help to lower the status of teaching for the degree candidates, chiefly by a disregard for teaching during the period of formal study and by an avoidance of certain kinds of teaching when the certified degree recipient takes a full-time position.

The disregard in its most innocent form is based upon a belief that subject matter preparation following a research design within a single discipline is sufficient for preparing a college teacher. And since such training is most at odds with introductory courses or other courses for the non-major, a wide expanse of teaching is neglected. In many universities where the majority of graduate students are trained, the lowest level of courses is turned over almost entirely to the graduate assistants. The relationship between this kind of teaching and subject matter preparation is remote, but the practice provides financial support for graduate students, relieves senior professors from the lowest level of teaching, and gives the university a large and cheap supply of instructors.

It is not hard to construct an argument that makes all this seem reasonable. A professor is not merely a teacher. In order to profess, he must give himself to scholarship. Nor should a person who has engaged his powers at such a high level be expected to teach beginning students. The custom of using graduate assistants as teachers fits well with these assumptions. Further, it may be argued that experience in teaching as in other matters is the best teacher. Thus, the system preserves high scholarship, meets the needs of both beginning and advanced students, and avoids the ill effects that might result if graduate scholarship were to concern itself with education.

Graduate Work and College Teaching

The argument has never been a convincing one to all members of the profession. The graduate assistants probably question it most, even as they are accepting the importance of scholarship to their future careers. Some of the questions that need to be asked are these:

With little or no attention to teaching in the graduate school, where does a college professor acquire skill as a teacher?

Is teaching a skill which develops on its own or which comes into being fully developed?

Are graduate students uniformly apt at teaching?

Is the development of a teacher assisted by giving the practice of teaching attention, respect, guidance?

What magnitude of scholarship disconnected from teaching can be justifiably supported by American higher education?

The recent surplus of Ph.D.'s gives point to these questions. A partial end has apparently come to the graduate school's inbred production system. The statistics on population patterns and college attendance seem clearly to say that the graduate schools must cut back or find markets other than the college and university for those who receive advanced degrees. But even before this crisis was reached, it was apparent that the specialized research scholar being prepared by Ph.D. programs did not fit the undergraduate college very well.

In her book *Challenges to Graduate Schools,* Ann Heiss has well summed up the present situation:

> Those who plan doctoral programs are faced with the dilemma of whether to educate scholar-teachers, teacher-scholars, or both. Usually they start with the basic question: Is any distinction necessary or desirable at this level? Until quite recently most planners rejected Newman's contention that "to discover and to teach are

distinct functions and distinct gifts rarely found in the same person" in favor of Huxley's view that research informs teaching. In either case, most graduate faculties have operated on the assumption that the process of becoming a researcher requires rigorous exposure to theory and practice but the art and skill of teaching "comes naturally" — or develops gratuitously when one is educated for research. Thus, the emphasis in most Ph.D. programs has been heavily weighted in favor of preparing students to discover knowledge, and only incidentally if at all on how to impart to others the nature and value of that knowledge. As a result, the American college teacher is the only high-level professional person who enters his career with no practice and with no experience in using the tools of his profession.

Another reflection of the disparity between graduate work and college teaching is to be found within the disciplinary associations. Almost a decade ago, the National Science Foundation supported the establishment of eight commissions on undergraduate programs in the sciences. Though the commissions focused upon different aspects of improving the undergraduate program, most were concerned with the ways in which graduate programs trained the college teachers:

From the Committee on the Undergraduate Program in Mathematics:

> It should be understood that no academic program or degree in itself qualifies an individual to teach effectively at any level unless this preparation is accompanied by a genuine interest in teaching and by professional activities reflecting continuing mathematical growth.

From the Report of the Commission on College Physics:

> There is a strong need to turn a much larger percentage of the creative effort of the entire profession to the task of understanding what we are trying to do in instruction, and how we may do it better.

From the Commission on Undergraduate Education in the Biological Sciences:

> The university is the only place where future teachers in universities and in colleges of all types can learn to teach undergraduates. If the job is not done by the universities, it is not done.

These commissions, unfortunately no longer being funded by the National Science Foundation, have less well-established counterparts in other disciplines. The Committee on Undergraduate Instruction of the American Political Science Association is an example, and *P.S.,* the news journal of the Association, now has a section devoted to problems of teaching. The American Society for Engineering Education goes back to 1946 under that name and to 1893 as the Society for the Promotion of Engineering Education. As early as 1901, the president of the SPEE, J. B. Johnson, was saying, "The time is ripe for men to prepare themselves expressly to teach in the engineering colleges." By 1912, another Society spokesman was criticizing the use of teaching assistants:

> The common practice of placing an inexperienced teacher in charge of a class and permitting him to drift until, by chance in the course of years, he discovers his inefficiency, is wrong to the individual, the student, and the institution.

The Situation in Biology and English

It is useful to draw upon the work of CUEBS, the Commission on Undergraduate Education in the Biological Sciences, and upon a recent survey of English departments in major graduate schools to give some details about the general university situation.

In biology, a survey of the 94 leading universities granting Ph.D. degrees revealed that 66 percent provided no special training to teaching assistants before they taught, and eighty percent offered no special course or seminar in any aspect of college teaching. To judge from the work of CUEBS, only a small but active part of the profession is clearly concerned with the implications of such training. Young college biology teachers, however, are acutely concerned. At a conference in Washington, D.C., in 1969, fourteen recent Ph.D. graduates who had taught for one year, nine graduate students now in Ph.D. programs at major universities, and fourteen department heads, faculty members, and foundation officials confronted the problem. There was unanimous agreement about the high quality of academic preparation in the graduate schools, and almost unanimous agreement about the deficiencies in the preparation of teachers.

The reasons the CUEBS report gives for the deficiencies apply to all disciplines:

teaching has a lower status than research

subject matter training is thought to be all that is necessary for the training of college teachers

the schedule is too crowded, the faculty too busy to give attention to teaching

"education" is a pejorative term in academia

strong conflicts exist as to whether teachers can be taught or how they might be

Nevertheless, at the Washington conference and at subsequent regional meetings, there was strong agreement that preparation for college teaching must become part of the graduate program. The CUEBS booklet, *Preservice Preparation of College Biology Teachers,* is an excellent discussion of the whole subject. Among the booklet's recommendations are these directed toward the graduate schools: 1) consider offering the D.A. or other practitioner's degree; 2) permit creative investigation related to the teaching of biology to be used as a dissertation; 3) improve the program for teaching assistants; 4) consider developing a seminar or course on effective teaching as a companion to the teaching experience; and 5) find ways to enlist the participation of senior members of the department in the improvement of the program for future teachers.

The situation in English is revealed through a survey conducted in 1970 for the National Council of Teachers of English of two-dozen graduate schools which grant about three-fourths of the Ph.D. degrees in English. The responses clearly indicated that the subject matter course work and research embodied in a dissertation constituted the formal preparation of most college English teachers. English graduate students did have opportunities to gain teaching experience as graduate assistants. Where course work or seminars in teaching were being offered, they were usually closely related to specific needs of the graduate assistants teaching freshmen composition or other introductory courses. Little systematic attention seemed to be given to development of the teacher as he or she was likely to be employed in an undergraduate college.

More than half of the schools indicated that many Ph.D. candidates had teaching experience as a major part of their training, and eight indicated that teaching experience was required of Ph.D. candidates. The most revealing general finding was that 17 of the two-dozen department chairmen or graduate directors responding to the questionnaire said they were not satisfied with the present program. A good many respondents indicated that the programs were undergoing revision, and some suggested the directions such revisions might take. The respondents' remarks are revealing, not only about attitudes and directions in English, but in other disciplines as well:

1. "We need to go beyond what we are now doing. The department has appointed a D.A. committee. In a relatively short period of six months, representing intensive study and work, the committee came up with a thorough and imaginative report. It held hearings among the regular faculty and graduate students and plans to have a conference of junior college faculty." (University of Washington)

2. "I should like to have one year's teaching a formal requirement for Ph.D. candidates." (Duke)

3. "We must set up a system of guided teaching in introductory literature with a one-to-one relationship between graduate-assistant teacher and senior professor, visiting one another's courses, talking regularly together, examining the rationale of the specific courses, and so on." (Ohio State)

4. "Like everyone else, we are uptight about teacher training, D.A. programs, student participation, etc. etc. A committee is studying the whole question of preparation for a college teaching career, and will make its recommendations later in the year." (Fordham)

5. "The third and newest option available is for graduate students to sit in on a section of one of our basic courses, following the methods of a given teacher and discussing them with him at intervals, and upon occasion taking over the class for one or two meetings with the regular teacher sitting in and evaluating the performance." (Yale)

6. "We are discussing possible changes." (Columbia)

7. ". . . in the process of revising both its M.A. and Ph.D. programs — in what ways it's too early for me to say." (University of Chicago)

It seems clear that forces are now exerting themselves to move graduate work to more responsible programs for preparing college teachers. Graduate students themselves are asking for better training programs, calling for course work, involvement of the senior staff, academic credit for teaching courses, and more professional guidance in aspects of teaching. The development of higher education as a subject matter area in Colleges of Education is evidence of growth in student as well as faculty interest. Efforts to establish the Doctor of Arts degree are also focused upon the needs for better undergraduate teachers. Whether the degree succeeds in establishing itself or not, the questions it raises will tend to push reform of the Ph.D. degree in the direction of better preparing college teachers. The economic situation, which may work against the establishing of a new degree, may be highly favorable to reforms in the Ph.D. program which might enable students to compete more effectively in a tight market. And finally, enough scattered, individual efforts now exist in the way ·of improving preparation programs that some general guidelines can be proposed.

Guidelines

Involving the Senior Staff

Foremost in the thoughts of many graduate students is the wish that senior faculty members would give some attention to their students' development as teacher. Supervision is not necessarily what they have in mind, nor courses in pedagogy taught by senior professors. Some students undoubtedly prefer to be left alone. But they do want from the professors they respect most some recognition that teaching is an honorable calling, that it can engage the full energies, imagination, and intellect of the brightest students. Or to put the matter in the way it often comes at graduate students: that the best minds don't necessarily go into research and that the less capable students end up teaching.

The ways of evincing such an interest are many. A list of four may do to suggest possibilities.

1. Involvement of senior staff members in lower-division, non-major courses. Such involvement need not mean all the senior staff all the time, but it should involve enough senior staff in enough courses on a continuing basis to offset the general pattern of withdrawal from the lower division as one rises in the professorial ranks. Nor does it necessarily mean that senior staff members should be teaching basic skills or introductory courses in routine ways.

Further, involving senior professors in the general college program is not just doing a favor to undergraduate or graduate students. It adds to the fairly small number of ways the senior staff member himself may renew his interest in teaching, break out of the ruts into which his teaching may have fallen. The major purpose of involving the senior staff is that of altering the value system that many graduate students resent, yet feel constrained to follow. We cannot expect graduate students to become excellent undergraduate teachers unless undergraduate teaching is honored by those at the highest level of professional achievement.

2. Taking part in team teaching of various basic courses and working directly with graduate assistants and less experienced professors. The clash of minds which can take place in such contexts is vital evidence that teaching matters. The willingness of established professors to be challenged and to be able to bring their knowledge and experience to bear upon a general subject can have an important impact upon students planning a teaching career.

3. Direct and continuing involvement in formal and informal programs of supervision or teacher training of graduate assistants. As things stand, such duties, like the whole program of preparing teachers for the public schools, are pretty much passed on to those — assistant professors and women — least able to defend themselves against the assignment. A program may be a very good program but it will still not be given the respect it deserves if it is carried on as something the department has to do rather than something that staff members in all ranks want to take part in.

4. Becoming concerned with education in its larger sense and with teaching in other contexts than the senior or graduate seminar. Today's students have caused a good many senior professors to become anxious about their teaching practices. The teaching relationship is too intimate a one not to feel the press of the catchwords "irrelevance" and "obsolescence." Student resistance to the traditional ways may bring professors to examine their own scholarly preoccupations in the larger context of social and educational needs. The concern for education outside the confines of a university has already drawn eminent scholars into concerning themselves with the high school curriculum in mathematics and physics. Project English was aimed principally at instruction in the public schools, but faculty members from colleges and universities were heavily involved. Nor should it be forgotten that the distance between faculty members at the major research universities and at small private colleges can be very great, too.

Public school education still suffers from the disconnection of college and university subject matter departments from the public schools. A well-established faculty member who ventured out of his or her department to experience public school teaching first-hand would not only have his own horizons expanded but also those of his graduate students who became aware of the experience.

Getting Involved

The important consideration in all this discussion is breaking down the separations that exist between graduate scholarship and undergraduate teaching. The suggestions made are not intended to apply to all professors at all times. Forsaking of all scholarship would in the long run work great harm upon teaching. But the separation of scholarship from a broad range of teaching has already worked much harm. Graduate students sense these separations, and a graduate program which would produce some approximations of the ideal scholar-teacher might begin by such a simple step as demonstrating that the senior staff cares about teaching.

The emphasis upon the senior staff is not meant to exclude or excuse junior staff members from such involvement. In thinking about the organization and operation of faculties in departments, the various conference groups have stressed (1) making the most of diverse talents and interests, and (2) maintaining a flexibility which enables department faculty members to move in and out of various necessary tasks. Implicit in these recommendations is belief in the ability of a department to operate rationally and democratically, in the necessity of defining and redefining a department's goals, and in using all faculty members to the top of their abilities to carry out these objectives. Such a concept is quite contrary to the aristocratic notions of a scholarly hierarchy in which the senior professors take on privileges somewhat in accordance with their age, specialization, and assertion of traditional rights. Part of those privileges was a freedom from teaching, a freedom which was to serve the common interest in furthering scholarship of a rare and valuable kind. More often than not such freedom has resulted in modest achievements in scholarship, very modest in the contexts of social needs, and at the price of failing to touch hundreds of thousands of students.

One emphasizes the involvement of senior professors because the senior professors have probably departed furthest from under-graduate teaching. But what is being asked for is an involvement of an entire faculty, without regard for rank, in ways that indicate an informed and passionate interest in preparing first-rate teachers as well as scholars.

Experience in Teaching

Among the replies received from the survey of graduate English departments was one from a prominent Eastern university which revealed none of the practices thought to be useful in preparing teachers. Yet, the department chairman said he was satisfied with the program. What appeared to be a stuffy defense of exclusively subject matter preparation was modified in one important respect: all advanced degree candidates were required to teach.

Closer examination of the reply both supported and questioned the department chairman's satisfaction with the program. On the one hand, the department apparently provided extensive supervision of the graduate student's teaching. With the exception of *in-service training program,* such supervision included all of the possibilities mentioned in the questionnaire: *preservice training program, student teacher assigned to experienced teacher, conference and consultation with designated supervisor, group discussions between supervisor and assistants, and group discussions in which many staff members participate on a regular basis.* The graduate students also had primary responsibility for everything in the courses they taught: *selection of textbooks, development of course syllabus or outline, final examinations, grading, and revising course or developing new courses.*

On the other hand, there was no indication of how much teaching experience was required, and a clear indication that supervision was primarily done by *designated faculty member or members* and *experienced graduate students.* Few full professors were involved in any of the activities associated with the graduate student's teaching experience. Most damaging of all, graduate students taught no courses except freshman English.

As a former chairman of an English department, I am suspicious of relying wholly upon teaching experience chiefly involving a single required course as a means of preparing graduate students as teachers. I have seen many such programs, and I have characterized the supervision commonly given to graduate assistants in English as largely defensive. The activities are not really designed to develop the graduate student as teacher, but to keep down the incidence of complaints among students taking freshman English. For the most part, this kind of teaching is as cut off from the teaching assistant's course work, from the major energies of the faculty, as if it were sub-contracted to a private firm. It could hardly help being cut off by the mere act of restricting teaching to one course at the most basic level. Surely graduate schools cannot long deceive themselves that freshman English is to comprise the teaching load of future college English teachers. Nor can they really believe that teaching freshman English prepares the graduate student for teaching everything else. What might appear to be a defensible program based on required teaching experience may really be the customary use of large numbers of freshmen to provide financial support for graduate students to enable graduate professors to carry on their scholarly activities.

I have been discussing a specific situation, though a common one, in English. Actual teaching experience under some form of supervision is probably the prevailing practice in English departments. Such practice does not rest upon a careful and enlightened examination of what would be best either for the freshman student or the advanced degree candidate. Its basis is economic and to defend the system is to call attention to the good features of a bad practice. The abuse of graduate assistants may in part be solved by the rise of collective bargaining, for clearly the assistants comprise an exploited class of workers for whom militant unionism may be the only recourse.

But practices which involve actual teaching under some supervision, common enough in English, are not common to the entire university. In the sciences, graduate assistants are much less likely to gain actual teaching experience. The graduate assistant often functions as a supervisor of labs, or as a manager of equipment, or as a general assistant to a staff member. Many graduate assistants find that this kind of employment leaves them quite unprepared to assume a full-time college teaching position. In addition, graduate assistants in the sciences often feel the effects of the distinction which places the "teaching" assistant below the "research" assistant.

One other general pattern of teaching experience will help illuminate the variety of ways in which graduate students are employed. In departments, especially in the social and behavioral sciences, where large numbers of graduate students are found and in which custom preserves very large lecture courses for beginning students, teaching assistants are usually assigned as section men. The staff member lectures to the multitudes once or twice a week and the section men take over for clarification and discussion the other three or four days. The responsibility the section man has for the class varies widely. At one extreme, the section man may have almost full responsibility including the assigning of grades. At the other extreme, at barbarous universities, the section man's duties may be officially recognized as "graderships." All the onerous work passes over to him, and none of the responsibility for course content, texts, assignments, or teaching strategies.

In sum, teaching experience covers a wide variety of practices, much of which fails to show thoughtful consideration of its functions as preparation for a teaching career. Much of the common experience produces negative effects: an over-exposure to the necessary drudgery of teaching, a sharp sense of the academic games to be played to escape such drudgery, and a disrespect for the teaching one is forced to do. Positive effects do exist. Graduate students given full responsibility for a course do find teaching exciting. As a group, they probably spend much more time discussing teaching among themselves than do staff members. And out of such excitement and exchange of ideas, graduate students do develop as teachers.

The Teaching Apprenticeship

But there is much more that could be done with that experience and much more that could be gained from it. Let me suggest some minimum considerations in shaping an effective apprentice teaching experience.

1. *Recognition of teaching experience as an integral part of the program for advanced degree candidates who envision college or university teaching as a future career.* Candidates headed for research careers would not be expected to have such experience, but, on the other hand, graduate students would not be casually employed as teaching assistants without much regard either for their aptitude or future intentions.

The aim would be to establish a vital relationship between subject matter courses and preparation for teaching. In the ideal graduate program, simply because most of the professors would be superb teachers and would embrace a variety of teaching styles, every subject matter course would be a course in pedagogy. As matters stand, the development of a graduate student into a superior teacher may mainly consist of avoiding the bad practices he has encountered in his graduate professors.

Graduate professors vary widely in their teaching effectiveness and in the degree of attention they give to teaching itself. Nevertheless, it is not too much to ask that some professors in a graduate faculty consciously think of their students as future *teachers.* A modest attention to teaching within the courses such professors teach can be a powerful incentive for students to develop as teachers. It also can bring about that continuing examination of what we teach and how we teach and to what purpose that is missing in the department's activities as in the graduate student's program.

2. *General reduction of the class hours taught by teaching assistants.* Most of the teaching being done now by assistants is only in part apprentice training for future careers. The half-time assistant-

ship has graduate students teaching too much both for the good of the programs they staff and for the good of the graduate student's development as a teacher. Until a department is willing and able to break the connection between economic necessity and the employment of graduate students, the training of graduate students as teachers will be less than it should be.

As a general rule, a graduate student should teach no more than one class per term during his first year. Ideally, he should probably teach no more than that at any time when he is pursuing a degree, but the realities seem to argue for acceptance of more teaching beyond the first year. Flexibility is probably more important than precise limitations. It is conceivable that every graduate program might have specific teaching quarters in which courses taught would loom large in the student's program and in which other course work or activities would be closely related to that teaching.

The necessity is to get away from the automatic assumption, particularly to be found in state universities, that the graduate assistant teaches half of regular faculty teaching "load" and devotes the other half of his time to scholarship or teaching. At the same time, the fear that teaching will interfere with the preparation of the scholar still persists in some graduate schools. Too much teaching certainly interferes. But teaching experience in itself usefully works against sterility in scholarship. Properly done — and this does not mean merely throwing assistants into freshman English while the regular staff retreats to upper-division courses and graduate work — apprentice teaching can be good for both the apprentice teacher and his students and for the regular faculty members who remain involved in that aspect of instruction.

3. *Provisions for graduate students to teach a variety of courses.* Too much of what is done now is aimed at staffing the lowest-level, most heavily-populated, departmental course. Graduate students could be drawn into teaching in many other courses at many levels in various useful ways. Such experience offers invaluable training for the college teacher. Within a variety of teaching assignments, a valuable integration of teaching, course work, and other activities might reduce the distance between subject matter preparation, professional development, and teaching.

Consider what might result if a teacher of American literature, for example, were to see his task not solely as a scholarly probing of textual or critical or historical aspects of a defined body of work but as a scholarly probing aimed at illuminating the general public understanding of a portion of the culture that a literature reflects. Such an aim would not settle for graduate student programs which consisted of a lecture course, a cram-course in Anglo-Saxon, a seminar in criticism and two sections of freshman composition. Suppose, instead, the graduate student's teaching assignment provided a continuing but shifting center for his academic work. Thus, he might bring a group of excited undergraduates into a deeper and broader understanding of the American present by his teaching a course which was being fed by his own investigations of the American past. At another time, Romanticism might be his teaching assignment and his graduate program would fill out his understanding not merely by exposure to a graduate course in the English romantics but by exposure to undergraduate students wanting to find out more about the romantic response to life itself.

Formal and Informal Studies in Teaching

Most of the above proposals would not be strongly opposed by many graduate departments. Difficulties in actually doing many of the things mentioned would still have to be overcome. But in respect to what graduate students should know about teaching and how they should gain that knowledge (aside from actual experience) there is much disagreement. Anything that smacks of "education" would probably arouse strong objections. And if a proposal were for "courses in Education," the objections would be intense.

To a degree, such objections are justified, for higher education is too course-ridden as it is, and the graduate school should be the place to get away from course work. Still, specific study and discussion of teaching and learning and the broader aspects of higher education as a career, even in a course, might not be a waste of time. Such courses are springing up, and graduate students, themselves, seem to be pushing for them.

At Harvard, Kiyo Morimoto in the Bureau of Study Council has conducted very successful seminars in which teaching fellows listen to tape recordings of teachers in action and through discussion gain insight into their own practices. At some remove from this kind of group work, which is an extension of the counseling situation, are various courses providing both information and experience. Michael Scriven, in the Philosophy department at the University of California at Berkeley has created such a course and is actively seeking to further other efforts along these lines.

Whether in a formal course or not, such work should carry credit, preferably in some kind of lump sum assigned to the teacher preparation aspect of the student's program as lump sum credit hours are given to the dissertation. Frank Finger describes a seminar in Psychology that he has taught for a number of years at the University of Virginia. The seminar takes in only students who have passed their prelims and deliberately maintains a "non-course" atmosphere. Wide reading of books and periodicals dealing with the broader professional aspects of college and university governance, kinds of higher educational institutions, academic freedom and tenure, history of higher education and of academic and professional psychology, fields of psychology, student rights and responsibilities, objectives of higher education, the professional marketplace, personnel problems, financial resources, and professional ethics are included. In the two semesters of the seminar, it has also been possible to give attention to the specifics of teaching and to conduct a teaching practicum. Professor Finger's conclusions, based upon the reaction of students in the seminar and reports of their activities in later years, are that such training has helped students enter into teaching duties with zest and has provided them with a broader concept of a professor's responsibilities without hampering their growth as scholars.

English departments have had much experience in informal seminars to meet basic needs of training large numbers of assistants. But the survey of graduate departments failed to locate any courses either within the English department or outside which dealt with basic concepts of learning and teaching. Richard Braddock, who has worked for many years with the training of teaching assistants in English at the University of Iowa, offers good advice for the formation of an informal teaching seminar. "Heavily involve your colleagues," he advises, "both experienced and inexperienced colleagues, in any program you have for helping your new instructors meet the problems of their first teaching."

Broadening the Dissertation

The kind of doctoral dissertation and the emphasis placed upon it has important implications for teaching. Don Cameron Allen's, *The Ph.D. in English and American Literature,* is not very respectful toward the traditional dissertation, once considered "ultimate proof of the doctoral student's competence," and maintained as "an original contribution to knowledge." The report not only recommends shortening the dissertation and making it more to the point but asks the question: "Does not good sense also suggest that something other than the traditional dissertation is sufficient evidence of a candidate's literary ability?" The passage goes on to endorse theses of a critical nature as well as original work of literary merit, both of which have been accepted by many graduate departments.

The way seems clear to suggest something other than the traditional dissertations as evidence of a candidate's *teaching* ability. It is a curious paradox of the literary scholar's aims and fulfillment that few of the many doctoral students trained in research remain productive scholars, just as few become writers in any professional sense. But almost all do become teachers, at least by the measures of what they are paid for and of what occupies their time. It seems wasteful, therefore, to put off certain kinds of demanding, scholarly work until after the student achieves the doctor's degree. The preparation of a good course involving the assembling and imaginative structuring of materials and carrying with it a clear sense of purpose and ideas for achieving that purpose is a task fully as demanding and rewarding as writing a research thesis.

The University of Utah English department now offers such a dissertation option. The option includes the actual teaching of the course under the supervision and evaluation of the candidate's doctoral committee. The Doctor of Arts degree at Carnegie-Mellon permits three types of dissertation: curricular, scholarly, or creative. "The first two types of dissertation, growing out of applied curricular or pedagogical investigation or out of traditional literary research, will demonstrate the candidate's ability to do original work on a significant topic. Each will relate literary scholarship to the teaching of literature. That is, the dissertation based primarily on curricular or pedagogical research will be consonant with sound scholarship and criticism of the literature involved, and the dissertation based primarily on historical or critical research will examine the implication of its findings for teaching."

Though the "teaching dissertation" might not be applicable to all disciplines, it surely is appropriate to many. Indeed, it could be argued that the research dissertation is not very appropriate to many departments nor to the variety of graduate students within those departments. The surplus of Ph.D.'s on the academic market has done more than anything else to call into question many of our assumptions about the makeup of a good Ph.D. program. The traditional definition of the dissertation across all disciplines is not likely to stand up under that questioning.

The Ph.D. Examinations

One last aspect of the conventional graduate program needs discussion: the examination or examinations which are the crucial tests for a Ph.D. candidate. It seems necessary to me to provide within the examination some recognition of a candidate's specific preparation for teaching. Perhaps the easiest way is that of asking the candidate to work up as part of his examination a short oral presentation of some aspect of his studies. If he is cautioned against making this merely an exercise to impress the examiners with his learning, such a presentation can give the examiners a sense of his ability to organize material, develop relationships and ideas, and get this across to a general as well as specialized audience. A good many examinations proceed in just this way. Its advantages are great for reducing the initial paralysis that can grip the candidate. More might be made of its usefulness in stressing the future responsibilities of the college teacher.

Appropriate examinations could also include actual observation by staff members with particular skill and interest in teaching, feedback from students, and counseling over a period of the candidate's development as a teacher. Such ongoing testing may be more revealing than the climactic examination which is to reveal at one sitting the competence or incompetence of a teacher. If a dissertation option of the kind just discussed is chosen by the candidate, the examination of a candidate's competence as a teacher would be taken care of there. If not, however, efforts might be made to formalize the examining procedures sufficiently so that the candidate would profit from consciously preparing for teaching as he profits from consciously preparing for the preliminary examinations.

Consideration of a candidate's fitness as a teacher might reduce some of the trauma associated with the preliminary examination. More personal examination of a candidate's development as a scholar and teacher is necessary along the way. No Ph.D. candidate should arrive at an advanced point in his program to find that he is ill-suited, for a host of possible reasons, to becoming a college teacher.

The Doctor of Arts Degree

The Doctor of Arts as a teaching degree is currently receiving much support. The cluster of questions asked in the Allen report about the feasibility of an "intermediate degree" reveals the difficulty such a degree faces. Department chairmen responding to suggestions for "improving the training of people who wish to teach but do not plan to do research" substantially favored a "degree emphasizing teaching and research" and "an intermediate degree between the M.A. and the Ph.D." On the other hand, almost three-fourths of recent recipients of Ph.D. degrees said they would not have taken an intermediate degree even if it would have brought them the same post and prospects they now have.

As yet, proposals for D.A. degrees are too few and too tied to existing practices and requirements for the Ph.D. to point the way to imaginative graduate programs for prospective teachers. Nevertheless, the D.A. degree may establish itself in American higher education, and there seems to be common agreement that it will be a college teaching degree. At the present time, the D.A. degree is being offered in only a few departments in a handful of universities. Somewhat equivalent programs under some form of a master's or doctor's degree title exist at probably a dozen or so institutions. Sixty-eight institutions are launching, developing, or considering the possibility of developing Doctor of Arts degree programs. Ten of these have been given substantial financial support by the Carnegie Commission.

American higher education may not be far away from substantial reform of the doctoral program. The economic pressures may dim the prospects for the D.A. degree just at a time when other conditions are favorable to its development. At the same time, the market pressures will operate toward reform of the Ph.D. degree, for the largest market for graduate students with advanced degrees is at the furthest extreme from the graduate school: the community college. These colleges, like the liberal arts colleges, will not succeed in shaping degree programs to their measure, but they will surely augment the forces demanding recognition of the importance of teaching. If, in time, the D.A. degree could gain a recognition as a degree different from the Ph.D. in emphasis and accomplishments, it would go far to increase the importance of teaching. If it could exist as a degree, like the M.D. degree, which was worthy of pursuing either before or after getting a Ph.D. degree, then teaching might gain more respect from the profession than it now enjoys.

Internship and In-Service Training

A good many plans for the Doctor of Arts degree emphasize the internship as the way of gaining teaching experience and as a substitute for the dissertation. Such plans do not differ greatly from the assistantship, particularly if the assistantship offered a variety of teaching and an intelligent program of accompanying studies.

The internship, however, does have the advantage of putting the candidate into an actual teaching context — a junior college or a liberal arts college — separate from the university in which he is studying. We have had such programs for years in the large number of candidates who have finished everything but the dissertation and who go out to full-time teaching positions while they finish their degrees. It is certainly better for a college if a new teacher has had a variety of experience as a teaching assistant. Serious consideration of setting up an internship program between a graduate school and a near-by college brings up the uncomfortable fact that very little exists in the way of in-service programs within colleges. Perhaps the formal alliance might help develop such programs, useful not only to the apprentice from the university, but to the first-year full-time teacher trying to find his way.

Another possible effect of an internship program would be to create some ties between graduate departments and their graduates after they assume teaching positions and with the colleges in which they teach. There appears to be very little feedback from graduates to the graduate departments as to the effectiveness of their preparation for college teaching careers. Such feedback is hard to obtain. Despite the orientation of students to their disciplines and departments, once they leave the university, they become the property of the alumni office, which in itself has little contact with the departments. The difficulty of obtaining feedback, however, should not stand in the way of trying to obtain it. Nor should it prevent a department from making use of feedback nearer at hand: from graduate student-teachers while they are still within the department.

One last consideration needs to be given great emphasis. If a critic were to take some graduate faculty members at their word and accept subject matter preparation as fully adequate for preparing college teachers, the question would still remain in all disciplines "What kind of subject matter?" Surely in that large part of graduate studies where college teaching is the chief occupation for those receiving advanced degrees, breadth needs to come into most students' programs. Even in the sciences, where specialized research aims are justified, the students planning to become college teachers could well afford to range more widely. If emphasis here has fallen upon specific ways in which preparation of teachers might be achieved, it is in part because existing subject matter programs are often hostile to undergraduate teaching and very seldom illuminated by an attention to what the nature of education, even within a discipline, might best be.

If effective teacher preparation programs are to come into existence, a series of meetings among recent graduates, graduate students, and regular staff members seem essential to planning. Over a period of time, a sense of what a department's graduates actually do as teachers might get across to the regular staff. Graduate students, inured to bearing an underground burden of complaint, would have a context in which such complaints might gain meaningful hearing. Even the most common of faculty practices, that of letting everything run along in its accustomed ways, might be disturbed sufficiently to make other ways seem attractive.

It is clear that departmental discussions are going on. The hope is that they will be illuminated by the actualities of teaching being faced by recent graduates and by the shared wisdom of the department's publishing scholars, dedicated teachers, senior and junior staff members, chairman and director of graduate studies, supervisors of graduate assistants, graduate students, and graduates teaching elsewhere. Through such activity, coherent, consequential, and effective means of preparing college teachers may emerge.

3. The Beginning Teacher

Most colleges and universities have some ways of inducting new teachers into the system. Norbert Tracy's dissertation study of orientation practices in North Central colleges and universities found that though "practically all" provide some faculty orientation, "only a few well-defined orientation programs seem to exist." On the whole, they are probably about as effective as programs for freshman orientation. And they probably have about the same impact — a small one — in relation to the actual forces of acculturation.

What do new faculty members need in the way of induction? What would be most useful to their future development as teachers? The San Francisco conference stressed the following as some of the answers to these closely-related questions:

1. Communicating in tangible ways the school's interest in teaching.

2. Explaining and clarifying the reward system.

3. Informing new teachers about ways of gaining knowledge and skills in teaching.

4. Acquainting new teachers not only with the department but with other departments and colleagues.

5. Giving the new teacher room to develop in specific ways, both related and unrelated to past experience.

6. Using beginning teachers in a variety of ways, but not using them too much.

7. Making conscious efforts to offset experiences which work against development as a teacher.

8. Providing specific, earmarked, reward possibilities.

9. Assisting the faltering beginner.

Communicating an institution's interest in teaching is an important part of the employing and inducting process. If a department or college has little interest in and little responsibility for teaching, it seems reasonable that it seek new professors who fit the department's non-teaching needs and who promise to add to the department's non-teaching strengths. But where teaching is both an interest and a necessity, the candidate's potential as a teacher should be given more attention than it customarily receives. Unfortunately, in the absence of an informed and intelligently operating placement system, neither the candidate's qualifications nor the institution's expectations get set forth in open ways that might lead to more of a match between the two.

Surely among the practices most ruinous to teaching in higher education is that described as "up or out." During the past twenty years of continually rising freshman enrollments, many major universities tended to hire large numbers of beginning teachers with the intention of keeping only a few of them when decisions on promotion and tenure had to be made. On the face of it, the policy gave the institution a cheap winnowing process for moving a department and the institution to a high level of excellence. In actuality, for many of the teachers kept as well as those who were let go, the practice probably deepened the cynicism already created by graduate work and experience as a teaching assistant. More certainly, it exacted conformity with existing faculty and traditions as one of the prices of retention.

The practice has probably contributed to the lack of attention given teaching in the graduate school, the lack of in-service training for beginning teachers, and the lack of career development programs within colleges and universities. It has helped support the operating principle that publication is necessary to survival and that attention to teaching by the beginning teacher is a threat to his job security. And it has not created for the beginning teacher either the freedom or the room to develop as a teacher. Further, it has created the kind of suspicion toward retention and tenure that made a judicious chairman at a state college say he could create a better teaching faculty out of those not kept by the major universities than by those who were.

All this might be defensible if the major universities were few enough in number and sufficiently unencumbered with undergraduate students to make a narrow and mechanical selection process adequate to the kind of faculty desired. But neither condition is true, and it has been at large institutions either dominated by or aspiring to high graduate school status where student complaints about teaching have been most chronic and severe.

It seems to me to be a much wiser practice and ultimately more economical to treat every appointment as if it were to be a permanent one. The beginning teacher is given respect from the moment he joins the staff, a respect to some degree from an entire departmental faculty rather than from those few younger colleagues who have made it. And he is spared the mixed friendship and hostility from those who haven't made it but with whom he will be competing for a future position. Respect, attention, time, assistance, and rewards given to a beginning teacher do pay off, ideally in the growth of that person during the years before he achieves tenure so that he can be given tenure with confidence that he will continue to develop as an excellent teacher and scholar. In the event he does not meet the one institution's standards, he still goes to his next appointment a good deal better for the experience. If he is too good and develops spectacularly, a better institution pays the lesser one the compliment of enticing him away. This is not postulating that all initial appointments will work out, nor does it deny the need for selectivity on the institution's part and the usefulness of turnover within a staff. But it does increase the emphasis upon making initial appointments carefully and upon using the probationary period specifically for development as well as for mutual observing and informing.

Informing The New Teacher

The first four items on the preceding list all have to do with informing the new teacher about his new position. Such informing goes on in various ways from the first exchange of correspondence. Candidates look at catalogues, ask colleagues about schools and departments, go about getting information on their own. In the interview process, department chairmen or deans furnish additional details. If the new position involves an interview on campus (and if we respect our profession at all, it certainly should), a great deal of informal and formal information gets transmitted.

Some of this information is about teaching, though a high percentage is probably about the details of courses, load, size of classes, textbooks, testing and grading, and the like. In the seller's market just past, a good deal of negative informing about teaching probably took place: what classes the new teacher would not have to teach, anticipated reductions in teaching load, assurances of rapid advancement to teaching upper division or graduate courses, to name a few.

What may be most important to keep in mind is that the informing process when the new teacher actually establishes himself on campus does not duplicate previous efforts. The beginner may know enough about the details of his new place and position to make a general orientation session redundant.

What seems to be most lacking in the period of acquaintance is any actual sampling of students and courses. It seems reasonable to propose that: (1) *candidates for positions appear as guest teachers in appropriate classes, or in other ways work with students as a part of the on-campus interview.* The purpose is not only to see candidates as teachers and to gain feedback on their possible appointment from students but, equally important, to give candidates an unmistakable sign of the department's interest in them as teachers.

Having such an established practice would also remind the department that the beginning teacher deserves more clarification of the reward system than just the customary expression of strong interest in teaching. Retention and promotion policies should be spelled out in writing, and each first year teacher should have a part in department-wide open review and clarification of policies and practices. Only by some such means is it going to be possible to reduce the misunderstandings which arise when theoretical policies are applied in an actual case of retention or promotion. The actualities — how things really work in the department — are probably more important to the beginning teacher than how things look on paper.

Thus, as a second recommended practice: (2) *departments should provide the opportunity, early in the first year, for the beginning teacher and his colleagues to engage in full and open discussion of the departmental and/or college reward system.*

Of less importance than the above, but still important, is (3) *the need to inform the beginning teacher about local resources for acquiring skill as a teacher.* This is more than pointing out what audio-visual equipment is available and how to get secretarial services for preparing classroom materials. It may be an identification of individuals with certain teaching interests or skills. It should certainly include passing on of information about special teaching opportunities, internal or external support of teaching, teaching awards, and possible paths of development.

Wise chairmen or deans, if they are not overworked, routinely do these things, offering useful advice and encouragement on the side. But there is no aspect of campus life which is not affected, and usually adversely, by communication which doesn't get across. Managing a flow of effective information involves cutting down as well as increasing the flow, making the most of informal exchange as well as attending to formal means. It is, I think, a major part of a chairman's responsibility, for it has much to do with the ways in which the department members function, and that functioning defines the success or failure of the enterprise.

It is particularly important for the new faculty member. For an accessible source of reliable information needs to be at hand to supplement and often offset the kind of information he will begin to get in informal contexts. Departments can fail to provide such socializing information. In small departments, a new member may find no easy and comfortable colleague relationships. It may take him longer to find them in the college itself. But regardless of the individual circumstance, the need to work at informing and to be sensitive to the various ways in which informing is taking place is vital.

In this connection, it is wise policy (4) *to provide for the beginning teacher identification not only with his or her department but with other departments and colleagues.* It is one of the best reasons, though commonly overlooked, for providing much more interdisciplinary work than we do. Every new faculty member should have an opportunity to teach with faculty colleagues outside his discipline. And though a necessary reorganizing of colleges and universities will have to take place before that can become generally possible, many ways short of reorganizing can be found to acquaint new teachers with other disciplines and departments. Inevitably, most of one's social and professional life will fall into the department; it is important at the outset to assist in developing other affiliations.

A number of small colleges provide such acquaintanceship by drawing together new and experienced faculty members from various departments. The current interest in teaching which moves toward the unstructured classroom or toward sensitivity training might provide a focus for bringing faculty members from different departments together. In a large university, the reappraisal of the graduate assistantship program might offer a similar focus. Providing an informal means of bringing first-year faculty members together with colleagues who have just gone through the first year or two would increase the chance of useful communication as well as offer experience beyond the department. Whatever is done, the deliberate "orientation" program or the discussion of theoretical "problems" should probably be avoided. Individuals learn more about and from each other when they are engaged in some specific inquiry than when they are brought together for some vague purpose thought to be necessary to their development.

Part of the reason for insisting upon colleague relationships outside the department is the feeling that departmental relationships by themselves may be dysfunctional. In a department where the young faculty member feels cut off from the power structure, the new member will undoubtedly get an effective orientation from his younger colleagues but such partial views may unnecessarily narrow the possibilities open to him. Departments, themselves, change, in part from the examples, competition, and pressures from other departments. And the developing teacher, in any case, should see himself as a member of the college and university as well as of a department.

Assisting the Beginner to Develop Teaching Skills

The discussion thus far has been largely of the realities of assisting the new faculty member to find his way into the department and college in ways that are generally favorable to teaching. The following discussion concerns itself more specifically with the other items on the initial list, all of which have to do with the beginner's development as teacher. It should be said that the "beginner" is not assumed to be only the new Ph.D. fresh from a graduate school. It includes women and men coming into the profession from a longer experience and other careers, teachers from the public schools moving into higher education, individuals with untraditional training and backgrounds, and large numbers still in progress toward an advanced degree. What is said may not be applicable to all these groups, much less to all the individuals within them. But there are, I think, some general considerations which apply to a wide variety of beginning teachers.

Beginning teachers need room to develop in specific ways both related and unrelated to past experience. Probably the majority of college teachers come into the profession with some teaching experience but most of it within the confines of introductory courses and beginning students. At the same time as the beginner may wish to escape confinement to the lowest level of courses, he may realize they are the only courses he has had experience in teaching.

More specifically, the new teacher in a basic introductory course in the sciences may find it a very different thing from his most recent graduate work. Before asking him to teach the department course as it has always existed, it might be well to give him some time to work back from his specialized knowledge to the general knowledge most useful for beginning students. In the humanities, the routine character of skills course might be altered if each new teacher were encouraged to move away both from what he may have been required to do as a teaching assistant and from the college course he faces. In all disciplines, the new teacher is often constrained either to fit into someone else's course or, without adequate notice, preparation, or assistance, left to develop his own within the department's framework. The new member faces a given curriculum and set practices which shape his practice. Far too little is done to enlist the new teacher, at the outset, in considering both curriculum and teaching in terms of what he might best contribute to both.

The department chairman must take care neither to give too many opportunities and load the beginner down with too rich a load nor to give too few and fail to use what a beginner is able to give. I think I would err, probably have in the past, on the side of giving too much. The aim was to open doors immediately in order for the beginner to have a sense of room in which to develop. There is nothing so sacred about the curriculum in any discipline that a new faculty member's sense of part of it can't be welcomed within the ordinary course structure. And there is nothing so precisely necessary about teaching methodology that a new man or woman shouldn't be encouraged to try his way.

But what if the new staff member has neither ideas about courses or experience in teaching by any method? I have a feeling that the best answer is that such a person shouldn't have been hired as a teacher, whatever other useful functions he may be able to serve. But until the graduate schools do a better job than they do now, beginning teachers who have thought little about and who have had no experience in undergraduate teaching are going to be joining college staffs. There may even be some inverse correlation between the man's standing in a graduate school and the standing of the graduate department within the profession and his experience as a teacher. Given a research fellowship in a department little concerned with teaching, the beginning teacher may be a very raw beginner.

Much that has been said about training graduate students applies here. The involvement of the entire staff in *teaching,* the chance to work with an experienced teacher, a variety of teaching assignments, are all good for the totally inexperienced beginner. In some colleges, a comparatively light load is given during the first year. In others, teachers with two or three years experience are deliberately singled out as most capable of assisting the beginner. Team teaching in a formal sense may be wisely postponed for the very new teacher, but chances to visit other classes and to be visited, to appear as a guest in someone else's class and to invite guest teachers in turn should be at hand.

Department chairmen have the responsibility to acquaint themselves with the new teacher's work, not only for what help the chairman can give to the teacher but for finding out how the new person's strengths may fit the department's needs. Thus, the department may be able to provide different patterns of development for different talents. Most important, an informed interest in the new professor as teacher is an invitation for him to work at his teaching, take pride in it, and develop it into an art.

Implicit in the foregoing discussion is the belief that teaching excellence can be recognized and to some degree developed. The project's work with evaluation (*The Recognition and Evaluation of Teaching*) is convinced that both are possible. Institutional policies and practices are shot through with the belief that research and scholarship need support in terms of grants, released time, and leaves of absence, but that teaching should be expected to develop by itself. The belief is particularly harmful to the young faculty member, for unless he already knows how to teach well, the college or university he joins offers few opportunities, outside of practice, to learn how. And though the right kind of experience, practice under the right kind of conditions, is undoubtedly a good teacher, institutions do not customarily provide either. It is my strong conviction that a faculty development program should include *provisions for specific kinds of grants — money, released time, or leaves — restricted to the faculty member with fewer than five years of service and specifically designed to (1) develop the individual's competence as a teacher or (2) contribute to the development of effective teaching.*

Evaluation of teaching, as well as of other faculty services, is also central to the problem of what to do about the new faculty member who appears to be falling short of a given department's standards. Customarily, this is not a problem. Out he or she goes, the department or college having ascertained to some degree of satisfaction that the person has fallen or will fall short. *The Recognition and Evaluation* booklet makes a strong argument for examining and refining the entire process by which faculty members are retained, promoted, or given tenure. The need to define criteria for teaching and to get accurate input as to performance is particularly crucial. Publication makes its own case, though as regards the person not being retained, the negative case, the absence of publication, serves as the most important measure for a great many schools.

If one looked at the matter in terms of investment in the individual, even for a probationary period of 4 to 7 years in the lowest ranks, less emphasis might be put on rejecting the unwanted and more on developing the beginner so that he would not be and possibly remain unwanted. It is a dreary reflection to consider the downward path of those who aren't retained for a variety of reasons at one place and another and who pass downward until they find a habitable level. No one institution in the course of that descent does much about trying to arrest it. Such redemptions may not be possible, but it is doubtful that colleges and universities try very hard to find out.

Let me give an actual example of a situation I became acquainted with this past year. Two young assistant professors in a large university department aroused much discussion at the department's annual review because of deficiencies in their teaching. Neither had much previous teaching experience as graduate assistants; both had excellent graduate school records; neither had published but the department did not place great emphasis on publishing if a young teacher were strong in other respects. Both were in good favor in the department, cooperative, conscientious, hard-working. The evidence against their teaching came from a variety of sources — students through informal comments and formal ratings; faculty by inference and information picked up from students; and from very limited direct observation. Still, the department faculty was in agreement as to each man's weaknesses and the nature of them. The one tended to be sarcastic or arrogant or condescending — students described the attitude in various ways — was inclined to demand too much and to parade his own learning — in short, to display the effects of graduate training in a prestige school. The other was, by candid admission of other instructors and students, dull. Some students are supposed to have come to the department chairman upset by the instructor's low ratings on the student evaluation, and to have said, in effect, "Yes, the guy's dull, an awful teacher, but he's a nice guy. Can't you make a teacher out of him?"

The question is a good one and the department decided to keep both — one in his first year, the other in his second — and see what might be accomplished. The easier choice, maybe the wiser one, would have been to let the two go and to let the next place they ended up teaching in worry about it. No very precise plans existed to effect the desired transformation. But the last I heard, the department was going to begin some informal discussions of good teaching among the two men and other members of the department with a keen interest in teaching. From that, the department hoped some other useful directions might emerge. The department felt that there was a reasonable chance the two would develop into effective teachers. If not, neither the individuals nor the department would be worse off for having tried.

Discouragements and Rewards

There are many experiences which can be defeating to the beginning teacher even when he joins a department under quite favorable circumstances. Overloading him with too many classes, too narrow a range of classes, and too unattractive a set of courses are common ones. Rigid separations between the junior staff and the senior staff do not fit the mood of the current generation of new faculty nor did they ever fit very well the concept of a democratic institution. Immediate piling on of committee work, particularly since the beginner is likely to get the least meaningful assignments, is not conducive either to teaching or scholarship. And though it may not be possible to prevent and unwise to interfere, getting caught up in departmental feuds and factions is something the beginner could well be spared.

On the positive side, there are a number of ways in which the beginning faculty member might be rewarded as a teacher. In the general affluence which has been enjoyed by a part of the professoriate in the sixties, it is forgotten that very little has existed as specific support for teaching. The beginning faculty member in the physical and social sciences may well have secured an outside research grant even before he joined the faculty; it may, in fact, have been a reason for his employment. In many departments in the scientific disciplines, the new faculty member may be joining an established research program. If none of these, there still is the research fund of the institution itself to turn to for support of research.

Few of these exist for teaching. The new faculty member in the humanities has some well-known outside agencies for supporting research — Guggenheim fellowships, ACLS grants, and in recent years the National Endowment for Arts and Humanities. But the breadth of support and the amounts of money involved are small compared with programs funded by private foundations, various government agencies, and the National Science Foundation for work in the sciences. Even in education, very little federal support money has gone directly toward support of college teaching and even less for support of individual teachers as teachers.

The neglect of teaching is related to the absence of a comprehensive view of higher education on the part of agencies outside individual colleges and universities and within the schools themselves. It affects the humanities most and the younger faculty member more than the senior one. For all young faculty members, however, little is to be found in the way of rewards that might lead him even to split his time and energy between teaching and research.

The Danforth Foundation Harbison Awards and Prizes for Gifted Teaching are the one comprehensive national program which singles out faculty members as teachers and gives both substantial cash awards and national recognition. In some individual disciplines, Engineering, for example, single prizes of this kind are given. Recently the Modern Language Association awarded certificates for teaching excellence to young teachers named by English departments. But considering the widespread public interest in teaching, and without even suggesting a comparison with amounts available for research, one has to regard the totality of these efforts as very modest.

Within institutions, sabbatical leaves and distinguished teaching awards are about the extent of efforts to directly encourage or to reward teaching excellence. Sabbatical leaves are still not to be found in many major universities, and the plans that do exist may or may not regard the improvement of an individual's teaching as justification for being awarded a leave. Teaching awards seem to be regarded with mixed feelings by the faculty. In Astin and Lee's survey of 1100 two- and four-year colleges and universities, 36 percent of the respondents reported the existence of institutional outstanding teacher awards. Colleges within universities used these awards much more than the other institutions, with junior colleges using them least. The survey revealed a great variety in titles, nature of awards, selection procedures, and selection groups. Perhaps this variety accounts for the equivocal way in which such awards are regarded by faculty members. Since the great majority of faculty members will not receive an award, the adverse effects upon them may outweigh the benefits to the few teachers who would probably function as superior teachers without receiving awards. The point of any such award must be its possible impact upon a large number of teachers who feel that this is a substantial recognition of teaching and worth working to attain. Even then, I suspect that many faculty members would be critical of the colleague who consciously sought to win a teaching award, though they might be quick to offer congratulations for receiving a substantial research grant.

If teaching awards are to be best used, I think the young professor group might be singled out for special consideration. The single award, however substantial, for a large university does not go far. A number of substantial awards to faculty members in their first five years might have much more effect upon encouraging good teaching and upon motivating beginning faculty members toward teaching. Such focusing of attention would also do much to arrive at reasonably precise and open procedures. Spread across an entire campus, one or a handful of awards too easily falls into a political game of passing it around from department to department, of atoning for past neglect of devoted teachers, or of satisfying the current interests of whatever group is dominant in the selection.

The teaching award may not be a very good means of encouraging teachers, however it is handled. Much more likely to be of use to beginning teachers would be funds available on application for work directly connected with teaching. The necessary scholarship, thought, and imagination involved in mounting a new course or trying a new method could then find a means of tangible encouragement.

The grants program within the state of Oregon's higher educational system is an excellent model. The present program developed out of an incentive plan for teaching in the form of money for teaching awards which was introduced in the legislature in 1965. Because of criticism of the teaching awards approach to instructional improvement, a substantial amount of money was made available in 1969 for a system-wide instructional grants program. The administrators connected with the program are convinced of its beneficial impact and presumably the faculty members involved in the 53 grants given during the first year share that belief. The University of Minnesota's Small Grants Program initiated in 1967 by the Council on Liberal Education is an example of a single institution program. Proposals must be directed "to the improvement of the quality of undergraduate education" and grants have ranged from $150 to $3300.

One need not ask for parity with research funds to argue for the existence of such teaching funds. There is little in the kitty in most institutions now. A modest beginning might produce more than modest results.

Discussing the Craft of Teaching

If we are to develop teachers, or incline the variously gifted in that direction, or to make the most of the born teacher looking for a full outlet for his energies, we must regard teaching as a practice more susceptible to development of skill than we do now. Perhaps we should think of it neither as an art nor a science, but as a craft. Or, as art often rises out of craft, look at the craft aspects sufficiently so that useful techniques, practices, notions, can be communicated to the new practitioner. One of the best examples of aspects of teaching which can be communicated is a series of informal talks at Western Washington State College by faculty members from nearby institutions identified as outstanding teachers. Last year, teachers from eight different disciplines talked about what they believed in and practiced. Their remarks don't constitute a textbook in college pedagogy. But recognizing the possibility of exchanging ideas and experience about the particulars of effective teaching might be the beginning of developing good teachers rather than merely passing poor ones on.

Here are some sample observations from the Western Washington talks:

- begin each formal class presentation with a general statement of what you expect to occur in the next hour or class session.

- begin each class presentation with something easy, something all students can grasp or accomplish (sound reinforcement psychology).

- proceed from the general to the particular or vice-versa, but know which approach you are following and let this be known beforehand or afterwards to the student. If you move from the informative to the theoretical or the conjectural, make this clear. Similarly for the reverse approach. Point out relationships.

- when opining, make this clear and request the student to do likewise. When speaking or pronouncing from data or what the discipline considers fact or "truth," so indicate and demand that the student do the same.

- don't expect the student to recite. Expect him to question, to draw comparisons, to pose problems for the instructor and his fellow students. "Questions . . . are the best single means of communication from students to instructor." A better device than a pop quiz is to ask the class to submit two or three questions rather frequently to be discussed in class. The questions provide both an indication of student comprehension of the subject and feedback of various sorts to the instructor.

- the instructor is under no mandate to deal with all questions. Some may be irrelevant or untimely. Some may be detours. Some may be beyond the scope or the intent of the particular class or its students. Some may be beyond the scope of the instructor. Don't brush them aside; briefly state your reason for not considering them. In many cases they become self assignments to the student or class.

- a working definition of "relevance" is a student-generated question.

- another definition is a personal experience or a professional concern or activity of the instructor. Another is a contemporary illustration, reference, or application.

- not everything one knows about the field goes into each course, though the temptation may be great. The instructor's obligation is to slice his discipline into appropriate sections called courses.

- lectures that duplicate text assignments demean the student and devaluate the instructor.

- texts followed absolutely suggest that the instructor is an overpriced commodity. An able professor is able to pick and choose and able to say why.

- a selected, scant bibliography or reading list, not a massive, waterfront collection of titles is the ideal, especially for undergraduate courses where the student is relatively unable to choose supplementary materials. The pinpoint list speaks loudly about the instructor's knowledge of his field and his aims for a particular course. The all-embracive list may dazzle or despair the student, but it says more about the professor.

- informal notes set a better atmosphere than does a script; they also allow for student interaction, interruption, dialogue.

- handing out instructor's class notes is much better than requiring students to take notes. Note taking should be kept to a minimum. Tell the student when to take a note; write the material on the board. Hand out a list of key points now and then, perhaps weekly. Don't despise mnemonics and other jogs to the memory.

- tape your class sessions now and then — hear yourself lecture, conduct a discussion, interact with the class and the class with itself. This is the way to listen to your organization, the pace of your presentation, the feedback that comes from questions and discussion. Try putting yourself in the student's chair and summarize for yourself what the hour's presentation and discussion did for you, or didn't do. Similarly, take your own tests assuming yourself to be an "A" student, then a "C" student. Can you differentiate via the test? Better yet, use a P/F basis for this evaluation. The purpose is to get the student through. You define the minimum competence levels.

- emphasis is a devastating tool of the instructor. Listen to yourself. What do you emphasize? What you mean to? Everything? Nothing? The best intentions are sometimes thwarted by inadvertent verbal clues or by the spacing or pacing of presentation and discussion.

- there is not enough supportable evidence for an instructor to assume students commonly learn more from discussion with him than from discussion among themselves. Make provision for student interaction. There may be days when you are not needed save on request. This perhaps is ego damaging but true. Let an able student group run the class for a period. Listen to the tape then compare it with one of yours. The same if you use graduate assistants.

- put attendance on a voluntary basis and quit worrying about it. Require attendance for pre-announced tests though — no reason to punish yourself.

- steal everybody's best methods shamelessly.

What of those beginning teachers who don't come to the college and university by the direct graduate school route, the married woman, the professional desiring to switch careers, the person from a minority group with an unconventional academic background? Probably the best general advice is that they should not be forgotten, either in the means by which new teachers are inducted into the college or university or in the general career development provisions for beginning teachers. Some recognition of the diversity of individuals and institutions being discussed in this booklet is given in Chapter 7, "Special Considerations," but the generalizations made throughout can achieve useful specification only if they are adapted wisely to specific situations. Rather than speculate on these individual needs and contributions, it seems better to bring together the observations made in this chapter and to set them forth as minimum specifications for that part of a faculty development program which would fit the needs of a wide range of beginning teachers.

A Faculty Development Program
for Beginning Teachers

1. Institutional policies would require departments to submit evidences of teaching competence or potentiality for all appointments except those fully assigned to research. Such evidence would not only include recommendations from those who had observed the candidate's teaching elsewhere, but reports on observations of candidate's performance in actual teaching situations within the department or college. Student as well as faculty input would be sought. Departments would not be permitted to make temporary appointments in excess of numbers required for projected regular staff needs.

2. The institution and departments would establish programs of information to the beginning teacher. These programs would not only give out information, but enable the new teacher to discuss such information with individuals inside and outside the department.

3. Each department would hold an annual discussion, involving all members of the department, aimed at clarifying for the new members the department's and institution's written policies and established practices on retention, promotion, tenure, and salary. This would be held in advance of the review of faculty personnel and would provide opportunity for revision as well as clarification of policies and practices.

4. Each college would establish courses, committees involved in some aspects of teaching, or other groups engaged in such activities, in which new faculty members from various departments would be consequentially involved.

5. The department chairman or an officially designated faculty member or group would go over the beginning teacher's teaching assignment at the beginning of each of the first years to arrive at the best possibilities for furthering the individual's development as teacher and to use the individual's interests and competences to develop the department's teaching effectiveness.

6. The institution would establish a program of Beginning Teachers Development Grants. Only teachers in their first five years would be eligible. Grants and awards would be publicized throughout the faculty and granted on the basis of specific proposals for improving the individual's effectiveness as a teacher or for contributing to the effectiveness of teaching in the department or university. Wide latitude should be given toward the kinds of acceptable proposals, and flexibility maintained in the kind of support provided. Needs of different kinds of beginning teachers as well as opportunities for other kinds of faculty development should be taken into consideration.

7. An institutional center for teaching should have as part of its central mission the furnishing of assistance to beginning teachers wishing to develop teaching skills. Such a center should also assist departments in working with teachers in need of such assistance or in establishing programs for developing teaching effectiveness.

8. The office of academic vice president or dean should establish annual programs involving the development of effective teaching. Programs might vary from year to year and include (1) discussions of teaching practices by gifted teachers from on and off campus, (2) opportunities for new teachers to demonstrate or discuss specific teaching practices, (3) reviews of departmental courses and teaching by outside teams, (4) rap sessions with students about the particulars of teaching and teachers, (5) development of specific innovative practices, new courses or inter-departmental alliances, use of students and teachers in different learning contexts and the like, in which the new faculty members would be significantly involved.

9. Institutions should identify highly effective teachers willing to give advice and counsel about teaching to other faculty members. The formal arrangements should be minimal, but the presence of such "counselors" should be made known to the faculty and, in particular, to beginning faculty members who may wish to seek such advice outside the departmental and administrative structures.

Though some of these practices are in existence and many of the objectives at which they aim are being pursued in the ordinary functioning of departments, department heads, and deans, I know of no place where such proposals are drawn together. Formal programs are not necessarily to be preferred to informal practices nor will they necessarily prove to be more effective. But the existence of a program may enable both administrators and faculty to do things which otherwise might not get done. The individual who hesitates to institute a new teaching practice may step forward within a program's framework. The cooperation often necessary to teaching innovations may be more readily forthcoming as part of a program proposal. Most of all, an institution needs visible ways of saying forcefully to its new professors, "Yes, we want good teachers, we respect good teaching, and we have specific ways of supporting both."

4. Mid-Career

Talking about the faculty member in "mid-career" brings up some of the profession's basic shortcomings in dealing with career development. Though in informal ways, the subject gets discussed extensively, few attempts have been made to conceptualize faculty development. The efforts are particularly lacking in comparison with the extensive literature on student development. Though the span of years is compressed, the basic task of identifying common patterns of development is probably no less difficult for college students than for faculty members.

Attempts to Conceptualize Faculty Development

Florence Brawer's *Personality Characteristics of College and University Faculty: Implications for the Community College* (ERIC Clearinghouse for Junior College Information, 1968) gives a useful review of studies of the characteristics of college and university faculty. Her conclusion that "they are few and they are inconclusive," is amplified by John Gustad's observation from a study done five years earlier:

> There is a considerable body of folklore about college teachers and a small but growing body of research. The folklore is interesting and sometimes informative; the research is informative and sometimes interesting. What we really know however is a mere pittance compared with what we ought to know.

The Brawer study cites a number of typologies. Busfield and Riesman classified academic personnel as (1) pioneer settlers, (2) pioneer adventurers, and (3) job holders. Alvin Gouldner gave

54

currency to the distinction between "locals" and "cosmopolitans" on a university faculty. Other researchers have tried to arrive at typologies of teachers. Adelson's *shaman priest* and *mystic healer* is one such attempt as is Axelrod's typology of teaching styles: *the drillmaster, content-centered, instructor-centered, intellect-centered,* and *person-centered* teachers.

None of the above comes very close to probing the way in which faculty members of different kinds may be said to develop. Nevitt Sanford in an essay, "Whatever Happened to Action Research," looks more closely at actual faculty development and bases his generalizations in part on interviews with faculty members. "It turns out," he writes, "that college professors develop as individuals in much the same way that other people do. Their development is progressive and is marked by distinctive stages, which are only loosely related to chronological age."

Sanford goes on to emphasize these stages: (1) **the achievement of a sense of competence in one's discipline or specialty, (2) self-discovery, in which the faculty member gives attention to other abilities, interests, and aspirations, and so expands his personality, and (3) discovery of others.** Ideally, these stages follow in order. "As in Erikson's (1959) formulation of stages, identity is followed by intimacy and generativity. Now the professor is prepared to use all of his skills in genuine relationships with other people; he may find it comfortable and enjoyable to take a father role with some students — those who can stand it or will accept it."

Ruth Eckert's work for the project described the faculty in terms of Young Turks, Middle-Guard, and Old Guard. Basically a chronological division, the characteristics of each group are supported by her various studies of faculty members in Minnesota colleges and universities over the two past decades.

The Eckert studies point out that the age group from 35 to 49 years constituted 47 percent of the Minnesota four year college sample. The remaining faculty were divided evenly between those 35 and younger and 50 years and older. With a small number of professors coming into the profession in the next decade, the middle-aged group is likely to remain large while the percentage in the younger group grows smaller and that in the group over 50 increases. In age, in university position and practices, and in experience and outlook, the gap is greatest between the younger and older group. Since there is little chance that much alliance is to be found between those at the extremes, clearly the major power resides and will continue to reside with the 35- to 49-year-old group.

Findings Regarding the Middle Guard

The following attempts to categorize some of the findings of the Eckert study:

Professionalism — The middle group appears to be more occupied with research and scholarships than either of the other groups. Some indications: the larger proportion of earned doctorates, the impressive number of publications and grants received for research, the more frequent off-campus consultative activities, and the greater expectation of research opportunities and the intellectually challenging life.

Background — This group had relatively few women; a more cosmopolitan makeup by birth; a higher level of education for their parents than the older group; and larger families than either the younger or older group.

Career Choices — The middle guard groups ranked between the old and young in the age at which they considered making college teaching a career. All groups decided relatively late, but the choice appears to have been made earlier by young faculty members. The middle group also differs from the older group in that fewer planned to become elementary or secondary school teachers when they received undergraduate degrees and many fewer have had such teaching experience. Young faculty members more often cited the influence of college teachers in shaping their choice of career, whereas older faculty members attached more significance to the advice of college administrators or counselors.

Current Employment — The public junior colleges have a significantly younger staff, with 37 percent below 35. In contrast, the private liberal arts colleges in the Minnesota sample had only 19 percent in this age category but led all groups in percentage of faculty members 50 and above. A substantial proportion (37 percent) of older faculty members in state colleges are still in instructor or assistant professor ranks. Few faculty members in this age bracket are to be found in the junior ranks at either the University or the private liberal arts college.

Professional Emphasis — Teaching and related tasks, such as preparation and extra-class contacts with students, receive the least attention, estimated in terms of time spent, from the Middle Guard. Teaching loads and associated tasks tend to be heaviest for the youngest group. Both the middle and older groups had a heavy burden of committee activities and off-campus services. At the University (in this case the University of Minnesota) the Older Guard has most of the key positions on faculty committees.

Professional Attitudes — Few in any of the age groups expressed a desire to put more time into teaching, though there was a general plea outside the junior colleges and especially among the younger staff for more time for research. Afforded a chance to suggest cutbacks in their activities, about a third in all age groups and institutions made no suggestions. Among the others, the most forceful reactions were against the time given to administrative or committee activities. (Parsons and Platt's preliminary study of the American academic profession supports this finding. They observe, "even the busiest researchers want to do *some* teaching and have *some* students," and note among the faculty a common weariness with committee work and administrative assignments.)

Job Satisfactions — In all groups, intrinsic satisfactions meant more than extrinsic ones. The younger faculty's greater concern for money, job security, and working conditions might reflect a greater emphasis upon extrinsic satisfactions. It is hard to tell, however, for basic working conditions have improved substantially for the older faculty, and many of the latter may also have become more accepting with age. The junior staff had greater complaints about low salaries than the older groups, but identified with about three-fifths of all respondents in complaining about poor facilities, excessive work loads, and administrative red tape. All groups expressed considerable satisfaction with their career choice, though the younger group showed a more qualified enthusiasm than the older ones.

Implications for Faculty Development

I will draw on my own talks with many faculty members these past two years to comment on these findings as they may bear upon the faculty member's development in mid-career.

First of all, their importance. Though institutions will vary as to percentages of faculty within defined age brackets, four-year institutions are not likely to be far off the Minnesota sample. The sheer size of the middle-age group suggests how dependent institutions are on that group's competence, energy, experience, and commitment. It may well be within this group that the decisive struggles are going to take place over the values that will rule in individual institutions as in the profession.

Second, the middle age group is particularly important in its attitudes toward professionalism and teaching. The Eckert studies show research productivity centered here (though they also show considerable maintenance of productivity into the later years), and give little indication that this group wanted less emphasis in research or more on teaching. The pressure to do research, however, seemed to be felt most intensely by the younger faculty member. Both represent a recognition of the established values and reward system in higher education. The most recent Eckert study shows the percentage of time given to teaching and other student-related activities declining by 10 percent during the years between the 1956 survey of Minnesota colleges and universities and the 1968 survey. Harold Hodgkinson, surveying the tendency of colleges and universities to move to more comprehensive institutions, concludes that "hours spent in teaching have declined for all five types of institutions; the more comprehensive schools show a more dramatic decline, however, than do the two-year colleges."

Against the implications of these data, it may seem foolish to see forces for an increased emphasis upon teaching coming from the middle group. Still, in my own talks with faculty, I am struck by the frequency with which some college professors refer to mid-career as a time of winning their freedom. If I interpret these comments right, mid-career is that time when the faculty member, secure in his competence, begins to see his profession in a much larger frame of reference. At its best as regards teaching, *generosity* becomes a kind of cardinal virtue, a generosity to other areas of study, to other experiences outside formal study, and to both colleagues and students. For that reason alone, it seems to be a promising time for capturing competent, influential, and still energetic faculty members for undergraduate teaching. Mid-career covers a long span of time (41 was the median age for the University of Minnesota staff in 1968, and about the median in the state colleges) during which competence and energy need to find various pathways for full expression. Surely, the self-discovery Sanford calls attention to could be expected to take place early in the middle years, and the movement to the discovery of others might follow upon it to enlarge a faculty member's teaching even to the end of his career.

As shaky as these postulates may be, I argue for them and draw some support from other characteristics of university personnel development. Administrators, in the university as elsewhere, are assuming important positions at an earlier age. College presidents, for whom an accumulation of years once seemed to be a requirement for office, are now being appointed at much younger ages. Derek Bok, Harvard's new president, is 41; Edward Bloustein, moving from Bennington to Rutgers, is 46. Robert Goheen, retiring this year at 51, was appointed president of Princeton at 36. What this means is that the public cries for more attention to teaching will come directly to young and early middle-aged administrators, most of them members of the faculty who have already moved into positions of larger responsibility and influence.

One other general condition can be cited as favorable to teaching. The forties, in a faculty member's academic life as in his personal life, are likely to be years of examining the achievements he has made in relation to the values he holds. How far have I come? How much time do I have left? Where do I want to go? These are the questionings which underlie middle-aged unrest and discontent, and which may have made possible more alliance between some members of this group and their students than between either younger or older faculty members. It may also have led to misalliances, the over-age hippy professor who seems to be as common a campus phenomenon as dogs in the Union. A sympathetic identification with youth's struggles, however, is not the necessary condition for getting a professor to re-examine teaching and its importance for him or her in mid-career. The necessary condition is an opportunity for change and accepted general patterns of career development which would make an intensive concern for teaching a real change for many highly successful college professors.

Teaching may also be pressed into service as an attractive possibility for rescuing some professors from a mid-career slump. An intensely competitive, scholarly career may not look as attractive at 45 as it did at 35. The need for more personal as against professional relationships, for more immediate satisfactions, for a more concrete sense of what scholarship can do may make a fuller commitment to teaching possible in these years. Nor need this imply that a person was not teaching before this time. It merely recognizes that scholarship, economic necessities, the building of professional respectability had first claims to attention. If one emerges from such conditions to one in which teaching, for a time, will be first and all else second, then some consequential transformation will have taken place.

Glenn Leggett describes one other common condition that relates to teaching at mid-career. "A teacher," he writes, "in his mid-forties usually has all his classroom techniques fully developed; he knows how to handle students, assignments, reading lists, examinations, papers, and lectures. He can coast along for a year or two on these techniques rather easily. But eventually the staleness of his preparation becomes apparent and he finds himself no longer attracting and keeping the best students and no longer able to have the exchanges with his colleagues that keep their respect. The staleness is fundamentally, I believe, his failure to keep re-educating himself in his discipline, and the failure to decide on priorities of direction." President Leggett's remarks are a useful reminder not to separate scholarship and teaching inadvertently. The one informs, invigorates, and renews the other, and it is a matter of shifting emphasis, rather than picking up and setting aside, which I have been discussing. Leggett's point, however, is somewhat different. He finds the failure to make a choice an invitation to drift. It is a serious failure, for it affects those members of a faculty whose broad competence has given them a choice of priorities among scholarship or teaching or administration, to name the most common options. The point is not that one direction is better than another. It is that for these faculty members, continuing effectiveness may depend on resolving the many questions of "where one really wants to put himself, not only professionally but temperamentally."

Differences and Similarities of Outlook

All that has been discussed thus far attempts to set forth certain kinds of development one may reasonably assign to mid-career and to consider how the possibilities relate to teaching. It should be kept in mind that any serious consideration of how faculty members develop would have to ground itself in the realities of a given institution. Ruth Eckert's studies, for example, show distinct differences between faculties of community colleges and four-year institutions in median age of faculty. Crucial differences exist, particularly between community colleges and state colleges and universities in regard to emphasis upon research, teaching load, and counseling of students. Considerable differences are to be found in family background, previous experience, and career plans of faculty members at different kinds of institutions. As Eckert's studies suggest, there may be more differences in job motivations, the variety of roles faculty are expected to play, and satisfactions from an academic career from college to college than from age-group to age-group within a college. It is well, then, to be mindful of these differences, probably most marked in the junior colleges, at the same time one is trying to generalize about common aspects of career development. There is a certain enforced commonality in the advanced education that almost all faculty members receive. In many respects, the more advanced such education the narrower it becomes. Certainly the shaping educational experience closest in time to becoming a full-time faculty member at any higher educational institution is one which takes place in a limited number of institutions and which proceeds largely through common programs and practices.

Amidst the variety of institutions and individual faculty members, conceptualizing faculty development is not likely to move toward exactness very soon. Nor is it necessary in order for individual colleges and universities to make effective career development efforts. For the faculty to be looked at is the faculty of a given college and not "the faculty" either, but individuals who might be helped along or saved some frustrations. The problem of improving teaching as related to career development is in part getting potentially gifted teachers into the profession and preventing their early or late decline, but above all, it is that of getting a fair share of already-existing faculty talent, energy, and commitment into undergraduate teaching. Those in mid-career constitute the largest resource we have.

Ideas for Attracting the Mid-career Faculty Member to Teaching

1. Changing the Routines

Change is one of the necessary responses one has to mid-life. Teaching, by virtue of its institutional practice, falls into accustomed routines. For the faculty member who feels restless going on in much the same way, changing the routines of scholarship and teaching may be a way of furthering his career.

An actual, and practical, example will illustrate what is meant. The 4-1-4 calendar plan has implications fully as great for the faculty as for the student. What I was struck by in examining the "Exploratory Term," as the January session is called at Coe College, was the variety that seemed to come into the curriculum. Something good must happen to a person's teaching, some boost given to teachers at mid-career, by such courses as: "The Many Facets of Dishonesty;" "Jane Austen Won't You Please Come Home!" (taught by a mathematician) or "Four Twentieth Century Artists: Charlie Chaplin, Jean Dubuffet, Duke Ellington, and William Faulkner."

The program at Coe is in its first year. The mid-career professors are heavily involved in it, and it seems to be working well. Other places have similar programs. Setting up and managing such an enterprise is not very difficult, though tangible institutional support is necessary. But an evaluation of such a program needs to consider its positive effects upon the faculty and teaching as well as upon the achievements of students.

Another example of changing routine is a modest beginning in the undergraduate college at UC-Berkeley in placing faculty members from one department for a limited period of time in another department. The internal mechanics are not hard to manage, and the person's presence in an alien department can be good for both the teacher and the department.

Neither of these examples of changing routines can be described as change for change sake. Both are reasoned responses to pressures from students and faculty to see things from a different perspective, in a different context, both essentials of learning. Both seem to work, and by no means do they exhaust the possibilities by which individuals and the groups into which they fall can benefit by breaking up the established patterns.

2. Programs of Exchange

In English at the University of Utah, an increased interest in the public schools has moved toward an exchange program which has as much to offer the university faculty member as the public school teacher. As yet, no formal program has emerged, but in the past half-dozen years, three public school teachers have spent a year at a time in the department and four faculty members have spent shorter periods of time in various public schools. In the physical sciences at the University of Arizona, a successful exchange program with the public schools has been in effect for a number of years. Once again, neither money nor administrative complexity stands in the way, and all those involved in the exchange — individuals and institutions alike — stand to benefit.

Though exchange programs exist to some degree among cooperating institutions, the opportunities are by no means as widespread or as visible as the size of the profession might seem to warrant. The visiting professorship is reasonably common; invariably, however, such appointments depend more on the visiting professor's national reputation than on evidence of high teaching competence within an institution. Thus, like many of the opportunities within the profession, visiting assignments go to those whose careers are already going well. What I am talking about here is for a wider range of opportunities for competent teachers in mid-career to see new places for a term or two by the mere process of going through with an exchange.

This is not idle movement for movement sake, though movement has its uses in fending off physical and mental staleness. It is a recognition of a change of scene which sabbatical leave plans and Fulbright grants for foreign travel have already endorsed. Sabbatical leaves are still not available in about 40 percent of higher educational institutions, and lack of funds is the commonest problem administrators have with leaves. What is being suggested bypasses the economic roadblock posed by sabbaticals. What is wanting here is the willingness of institutions to seek out other cooperating institutions, the establishing of some kind of regional or national network that would make an exchange program possible.

3. Institutional Support

Though the above suggestions would require little money or even institutional commitment, career development should not be seen in just those terms. If mid-career faculty members are to be attracted to opportunities, are to set examples for younger faculty, are to resist keeping to the path of maximum personal advantage, institutional efforts at career development must not be built solely upon faculty good will.

Few institutions put any sum of money into faculty development, and that, surely, is the first step. If we are to enhance the career of the college teacher, then a definite percentage of the budget — ½ of 1 percent, 1 percent, 3 percent — should be earmarked for that purpose and be kept from disappearing in the budget cutting process.

If that were done, many specific matters of support might follow. It is not enough, for example to have a teeming enterprise called the audio-visual department which can become one man's pride and few faculty members' supporting arm. Classrooms, themselves, need attention as places for learning, not only in getting equipment that works into them (and which does not have to be transported from someplace else) but in general matters of size, light, air, and acoustics. Administrators need some impetus for coming to faculty members in active support of teaching rather than waiting to respond to some request that will probably have to be turned down. And faculty members, themselves, need some obvious and potent signs that an attention to teaching will pay off, not just in the temporary support given to an ingenious proposal but in the long term regular support shown in rank, salary, and institutional respect.

4. Encouraging Innovation

Innovation is one of those cant words for education today. Few really come to grips with it. No one need fear it, for innovation always proceeds at a slow pace. One ends up opting for innovation despite the idle usage of the word and despite the company he may be forced to keep if he becomes innovative.

Nevertheless, the need to find new ways to get at old and new problems in teaching and learning is a real need. As it affects the faculty member at mid-career, innovation may be a way of renewing his interest in teaching or in finding new interests that could almost become a new career.

What kind of innovations promise the most for teaching? And what can mid-career faculty members give, what benefits can they get, from these innovations?

It is not to the point to enumerate the various kinds of innovations going on in higher education. If one were to set about describing all the innovations in teaching to be found within the nation's colleges and universities, he would probably end up with an impressive body of material. On the other hand, if his aim were, as mine has been, to examine teaching as it affects the majority of students, he would probably not be very impressed with the actual impact of innovative teaching. But from either perspective the observer would have to agree that in some particulars changes have taken place and probably will continue. Grades, classroom structures, teaching methods, living-learning arrangements are some of the areas in which important changes have taken place. The cluster college, the university without walls, the external examination, the three-year B.A. degree program are more comprehensive innovations.

Obviously, there is enough ferment going on now to give the mid-career professors ample opportunity to try something new or to join forces with these already embarked on an innovative program.

5. Sub-colleges

Let me expand on only one example. The formal cluster college has a fair chance, I think, of being a widely adopted device to meet the need for smaller academic communities than are to be found in large universities and colleges. It is also a way to meet students who profit by being identified with a special program, whether it be honors, black studies, environmental studies, or any of a number of possibilities. Large institutions do not really need bricks and mortar, departments, degree programs and the like to create, not one, but a good number of working "collegial" units. In fact, buildings and formal programs would work against the informal and transitory nature of such units, qualities that need to be preserved.

At the minimum, what is needed are numbers of faculty members from various disciplines willing to work together to offer sufficient courses, outside activities, and objectives to give the collegial unit an identity. Mid-career faculty members are crucial to such arrangements. For they are less subject to the pressures of the conventional reward system which may penalize a younger teacher's departure from the ordinary departmental affiliations and scholarship. At the same time, chances for a limited number of faculty to work within a collegial structure which might to some degree reflect a larger philosophy of education would be particularly attractive to mid-career faculty. Many faculty members today share the students' sense of being cut off from satisfying ends. In any teaching which processes large numbers of students, the faculty member experiences a loss in the knowledge of how he may be affecting any one student and of what happens to any large number of his students. The working out of effectively functioning sub-colleges, collegial units, as I have called them, is certainly not as easy as this brief sketch may suggest. But it is an innovation worth exploring and one which could not likely get off the ground without leadership and participation from faculty members in mid-career.

A footnote to these discussions needs to be added. I think there is a certain "ad hocness" coming into university management. Alvin Toffler's *Future Shock* has given the idea currency. University committees might well do better if they were set up for specific purposes and terminated when their purposes were achieved. Faculty members, too, are affected by a climate in which commitment to one career over a life time doesn't seem to be the most attractive of prospects. What might not be attractive as a longterm commitment, however, might be quite attractive for a limited period. Universities, then, might make the most of this mood and enlarge the opportunities for faculty members to move in and out of specific assignments. Undergraduate teaching, within or outside an experimental context, might be something mid-career faculty members would wholly devote themselves to for a number of years if it were clear that they could turn to some other aspect of professional responsibility after a defined period.

All institutions, then, should provide ways for a large number of faculty members in mid-career to emphasize different aspects of their professional development for limited and specified periods of time.

Barriers to Faculty Development

"Current faculty members," Ruth Eckert writes, "to a greater degree than their colleagues a dozen years ago, tend to view the campus as a place for pursuing their own studies and achieving their own personal and professional development, rather than for promoting such growth on the part of students." I fear this is generally true, and I would like to end this chapter by discussing some of the barriers, self-imposed, professional, and institutional which may stand in the way of development of the mid-career teacher.

The self-imposed barriers to sustained effectiveness of teaching or renewed attention to teaching at mid-career are many. Foremost, of course, is that we tend to perform in routine ways those tasks we must do but to which we are not, temporarily or permanently, deeply committed. Even the teachers who respect undergraduate teaching, who do it well, suffer from such inattention. Perhaps that is why so much emphasis in this discussion of the teacher at mid-career is placed on finding new contexts, breaking into routines, providing change.

If we are to have large numbers of teachers who can teach well and who will give full attention to undergraduate teaching for even limited periods of time, we must provide a respect for teaching which leads to tangible recognition and support of good teachers who give it their all.

Second, undergraduate teachers do have some legitimate fears that a shift of attention to teaching may slight scholarship, that in time they will become stale as teachers because they have become stale at scholarship. Once again, let us emphasize the complementary nature of scholarship and teaching wherever they can be complementary. I do not think this means finding ways that each faculty member can keep his specialized research interests and somehow usefully impose them on the undergraduate student. In the hands of a skillful teacher even this is possible, but I suspect more is changed in the nature of that research, method and substance, than the scholar is aware of if he is getting across to the general undergraduate student. The challenge is to a trivial scholarship which is not only ill-suited to the undergraduate but to almost any living being other than the scholar himself. The institution should provide in its faculty development program ways of assisting professors to move between the role of scholar and teacher. The year it may take to write a book is generally respected as worth both the university's and the faculty member's investment. The three months or six months to prepare a new course is not. Worse, the year produces a countable product, useful for any number of years at the weighing in for rewards and benefits. The course, once taught, tends to disappear among the other catalog offerings. I am not arguing that the book and analogous scholarly productions can't be potent teaching devices. But the profession's tendency to honor the publication of specialized scholarly work and to disregard the writing of textbooks, without much regard for the quality of either, is an example of general failure to recognize important relationships between scholarship and teaching.

If we are to have both teaching and scholarship and if they cannot be accomplished precisely at the same time, then we need to make it possible for faculty members to do both without one working more than momentary hardship on the other.

Third, the mid-career teacher is probably very conscious of his standing outside the university. Teaching is not a route to national recognition. And though national recognition is not necessary to a satisfying career, the presence of scholarship, of professional associations, of a national market for professors makes it hard to escape that measure. At early mid-career one is either on the way to establishing a national reputation or he or she is beginning to settle for local status. The situation is not that pat, obviously, but a desire to engage in those activities which establish or enhance a national reputation does stand in the way of a teaching commitment whose effects are likely to be local. On the other hand, mid-career is also that time when those who haven't made it in the outside world settle for teaching and perhaps a dilettantish scholarship. Neither condition is very good for promoting high excellence in teaching.

Here, I think, help must come from outside, from the disciplinary associations, from foundations, from the Office of Education, perhaps.

Every disciplinary association should have an active arm primarily concerned with teaching and effective in establishing means of national recognition for effective teachers.

Consortia of colleges can provide an outside context in which excellent teachers can be identified, usefully exchanged, and used within the consortium to improve teaching. The Danforth foundation's national award for gifted teaching has set the pattern, but the ten to twenty teachers it singles out each year go only a little way in giving teachers wider visibility.

Finally, the university or college could well invest some of its professional expertise in trying to understand how student and colleague relationships affect teachers. We know from a number of studies that the kind of students to be found in a college or university has a strong influence upon a young teacher's change of position. We know satisfactions with colleagues and students rank high among job satisfactions of established faculty. We also know that such relationships go sour, particularly noticeable in the present student climate. Similarly, we know that colleague relationships tend to be self-reinforcing. Those who are interested in teaching tend to run with others who are interested, and the group itself tends to identify and reinforce the already successful teachers. These are all reasons for giving assistance to teachers who may be frustrated by students or limited by colleagues.

An adequate career development program would get students and faculty, faculty and faculty, involved in ways that could lead to overcoming bad relationships and establishing good ones.

Perhaps only a small number of the above suggestions could be put into effect by any institution. Some of the ideas would not work out. Some of the problems involving career development would defy national efforts at solution. But institutions have not given much attention to career development, in general. During the middle years, when everything is likely to run along O.K. if you don't think about it much, both the teacher and teaching suffer most inattention. Benign neglect may be better than meddlesome intervention. It is probably not better than a reasonable attempt to examine how teaching goes with the majority of a faculty and to seek ways of making it go better.

5. Later Years

One of the three objectives of the Project to Improve College Teaching was to deal with the problem of the professor of "markedly diminished effectiveness," a phrase that tries to disguise what more direct academic usage has long called "the deadwood problem." Neither term indicates the complexity of the problem nor suggests the many kinds of individuals it may describe. The existence of deadwood (and it probably does exist on most campuses) reflects both ways, not only on those who may have become deadwood but on those who identify it in that way. At the same time one is identifying infirmities in one part of the academic body, he may be revealing callousness in another. The two are probably more closely related than it might seem.

Though the subject is discussed here in connection with the later years, any faculty age group at any time varies widely in its effectiveness. It is partly to dispel the notion that deadwood is only to be found among the senior faculty that we face that stereotype bluntly. Whether we use harsh or euphemistic terminology, what is being confronted is that condition which marks a noticeable decline from a previous level of performance. It may happen at any time in a career; it need not be a permanent condition; it may respond to diagnosis, treatment, and prevention.

Robert Helbling, chairman of the foreign languages department at the University of Utah and author of a paper on deadwood for the Washington conference, called for an emphasis upon a *developmental* rather than a *judgmental* system for faculty personnel. Preventing faculty deterioration is preferable to trying to cure it. "A 'programme of action' in this area," he writes, "can obviously not be divorced from reflections on the psychology of the teacher, the process of aging, the rapidly changing student and administrative moods, the effect of the tenure and seniority systems on classroom effectiveness, the teacher's personal commitment to his calling, and the interaction of the needs for self-fulfillment and security in the teacher's career."

A "Psychology of the Teacher"

Professor Helbling's list provides a sound basis for discussion. What he means by the "psychology of the teacher" can best be expressed in his words: "Though pedagogy is admittedly an old science (of sorts), what we might call the 'psychology of the teacher' is to my knowledge still a relatively untrodden field. I am not about to give a propaedeutic to such a psychology — I have none up my sleeve — beyond asserting that laymen and professionals alike seem to underestimate the degree to which teaching makes demands upon the total personality of an individual. Manifestly, teaching is not only a matter of method, though it is this also. It is rather a matter of complete self-investment. And since the self of the teacher needs the kind of constant reassurance which is existentially hard to come by — the favorable judgment of others — the investment is risky. To teach is to live dangerously. Psychologically, it is not the kind of secure job that the layman thinks it is and many Ph.D. candidates seek, though the physical risks are small and the paychecks come in regularly. Teaching requires a constant self-confrontation — a rather disturbing task."

Obviously, understanding what inner drives commit a person to teaching in the first place and what causes him to carry out that commitment in various ways during his career are vital matters. A chairman who would function well must have considerable gift at divining such motivations, willingness to inquire where divination stops, and the ability to act wisely on his guesses and knowledge. The chairman, more than anyone else falls into the role of faculty counselor, though he is also the one most likely to get locked into grim battles with individual faculty members.

While stress is being placed upon the chairman as the one to master the elements of the psychology of teachers, in some instance he may be precisely the wrong man to give advice or to turn to for counsel. The chairman must make the hard decisions, chiefly on salary and teaching assignments for the older faculty member. It may be useful, and advisable within a large department, to have some other place — a personnel committee, for example — to which a staff member, senior or not, could turn. In small colleges and large, where department relations are too intimate or too marred by divisions of various kinds, the dean's office often becomes the place where counsel is sought. What is important for the senior staff member is to have avenues clearly identified so that turning to someone for counsel is not interpreted by the man himself as an admission of weakness, a sign of failing competence.

Discussing the possibility of a "faculty counselor" raises much uneasiness, most of it well founded. Something short of a professional counseling office is probably called for. But it would be useful to have a number of faculty members identified in informal ways as those to whom faculty members could go for advice and counsel. They would not be identified so much for their credentials as clinicians (though professional clinical help should be available) as for the respect they enjoy among their colleagues within the university and the interest and skill they have in working with teachers.

The task of working with senior staff members is made more difficult under present systems of rotating chairmanships. The senior man who had long years to become acquainted with department members may not be the chairman or hold the chairmanship very long. It will often fall to a man less well-acquainted with senior staff, and one who because of his comparative youth may treat senior staff too easily or too harshly. Any chairman can use help in such matters, and a personnel committee, as mentioned above, or an executive committee involving young members of the staff as well as those nearing retirement may be necessary to add collective understanding to that of the individual serving as chairman.

The Consequences of Aging

The committees on career development, though they included individuals who were close to retirement, developed no extraordinary wisdom about the particular needs and frustrations, the mental set, of older faculty members. There is a large literature on aging to be drawn upon, though a knowledge of the teaching environment, of the past background of a particular faculty member, and some willingness to be generous in one's judgments are probably as important as grounding in general psychological understanding. It should be noted that the problem of "competence loss," as Saul Gellerman identifies it in *Management by Motivation,* is not a problem unique to higher education.

"Competence," Gellerman writes, "is, after all, a relative rather than an absolute quality. It is a matter of being able to do what is expected of one. But these expectations change, and sometimes the things one is able to do change too — in either direction. So competence itself is essentially changeable, not fixed, and we can reasonably expect it to fluctuate to some extent during the course of any man's career. Nevertheless, we have traditionally regarded competence as being rather like a beard; that is, something not acquired until adulthood and never really lost thereafter. Regrettably, it is becoming increasingly clear that competence is more like the hair on top of a man's head, in the sense that it is not necessarily there to stay."

What either a practical or theoretical grasp of psychology tells us is that age has different impacts on different individuals and that the term "deadwood" conceals many kinds and causes. Perhaps a useful basic distinction — if we were able to make it fairly — is between an involuntary loss in effectiveness and what might be regarded as a willful loss. We know that some of the effects of aging have marked consequences for teaching. The loss of energy, for example, is a serious loss, for teaching makes great demands on energy. An individual, drained by demands which remain too heavy or worn out at a comparatively early age, would seem to be suffering from an involuntary loss of effectiveness. On the other hand, a turning of interest away from teaching, a preoccupation with matters inside and off campus to a noticeable neglect of teaching, might fairly be regarded as willful. There is probably no easy way of dealing with either one or the other, but attempting to understand basic causes even along the lines of this crude division is useful to finding ways to meet specific problems.

It is also well to give careful considerations to the career pattern of a senior professor who may appear not to be functioning effectively. Deadwood probably can be found at all ages; it is connected with age in part because a long, apparently satisfactory, commitment to an institution makes a decline seem more marked and action more difficult. The ineffective professor may be the end result of a long decline, and remedies might be sought in examining the details of that decline. Or, at another extreme, it may appear with some suddenness, making one search for some peculiar condition that would explain a sudden reversal of drive or direction.

If we would understand the psychology of the teacher of markedly diminished effectiveness, we are necessarily obliged to pay more attention to the psychology of the teacher at all stages in a career. And if we learn something from that understanding, it is probably that a wise and continuing and non-punitive attention to career development is one of the best ways we have of minimizing the effects of old age.

For aging has its consequence for teachers whether they function well or poorly. The chronically ill but still able to function are probably less widely distributed through the older ranks of the professoriate than through the general population. The physical demands which make men and women in many occupations seek other work as a result of ill health are not that great in teaching. On the other hand, fatigue, mental and physical, should not be shrugged aside as unimportant in the teaching profession. Perhaps because teaching is inside, sedentary work with flexible hours and stretches of time useful for recuperation, it may permit the person with chronic or recurring health problems to maintain his position. However accurate this speculation, ill health associated with aging must be reckoned with as a cause for decreased effectiveness.

Commonly, I think, the profession tends to treat such individuals charitably, if not generously. Though health and hospitalization insurance are common fringe benefits, sick leave plans are not. Mark Ingraham's survey of fringe benefits indicates that 60 per cent of institutions have no sick leave plans. Often, the faculty member's absence for illness is covered within a department by cancelling courses or having them covered by other staff members. In such situations, it is no wonder the conscientious faculty member tries to keep functioning even when he has good cause to seek medical help. And though few administrators would fail to sympathize with someone plagued with ill health, the means to do something about it, in terms of firmly established leaves for reasons of health — may not exist. The matter of adequate sick leave provisions is one any college and university can look to, should look to, if the administrative sensing apparatus detects an abundance of deadwood.

But ill health in a visible, physically damaging way is but one consequence of aging. Consider the general flattening out of opportunities, the long stretch of time between a person's retirement and his achievement of rank, competence, and status. For some faculty members, this period may become a void. Job offers diminish; new fashions arise in scholarship and artistic creation; the action within the university shifts to the younger faculty. The rank structure does not offer a titular advance beyond that of professor.

Work in progress often keeps a faculty member conversant with some part of his discipline, though it is a fair bet that the scholar who has not produced in mid-career will not become a producer in late career. Even for the producing scholar, such attachments may not necessarily augur well for teaching as retirement approaches. With less energy to be distributed and with fewer years to complete work, the need for economy in teaching may become more intense. In a general way, the needs which drive younger men no longer exert as much force. Regardless of what fulfillments one has held up to himself in his youth, the time comes when they are either sufficiently achieved or their non-achievement sufficiently rationalized to reduce their urgency. A carefully devised system of career development would seek to provide ways of enhancing teaching opportunities for the older teacher without lowering the quality of instruction.

At Colgate University, Provost Frank Wallin makes it a practice of his office to interview all faculty members as they move into their sixties. Neither their university lives nor their actual lives are over, but anxieties about both may cause individuals to welcome an invitation to talk and, what is more important, welcome an extending of opportunities to use these last years both productively and satisfyingly. Such coming forth in non-crisis situations is important for administrators who work with scholars and teachers who are independent in outlook but often dependent upon institutional encouragement and support. Discussion of how a professor may best function as a teacher during his last years may be beneficial to the students as well as to the faculty member.

There are, after all, some great advantages to having experienced more life, read more, seen more, even forgotten more. Age is properly associated with wisdom, even though there may be foolish old men and women aplenty. Why shouldn't it be standard practice for a university to seek out the wisdom of its older faculty members? Some will have reached that point where whatever they teach is touched by wisdom. But many may have experienced the isolation of old age, the fears, even the embitterment which makes it not worth the effort to gather their accumulated knowing and experiencing together. Or the evidence of modest achievements which can no longer be disguised by promise yet to be realized may cause, if not a retreat, a reserve which will not bring one's best self forward. In both instances, the system and those offering guidance within it might think in terms of "promising older men and women." Structure may be more important to provide for these individuals than for young people who can find their own structures.

A good teacher, not necessarily a great one, may be properly hesitant to launch forth as a spouter of wisdom in his later years. But it is not too much of a hazard to have the system deliberately try to tap the wisdom that may reside in the older faculty. At the least, this attempt should encourage some faculty members to break away from

course and discipline structures to confront broader topics and in a
conversational mode. The "university professors" should not be a
recognition that goes exclusively to venerable faculty members on
the edge of retirement — it should include teachers from all ranks —
but it should be conspicuously available to teachers whose age gives
them some claim to wisdom as well as to mastery of a subject.

Students and the Older Teachers

When we talk about making more opportunities for teaching for
the older professor, we must consider the effects that students have
upon their teachers. In the Gaff-Wilson report, "The Teaching
Environment," based on a study of faculty attitudes, students were
one of the principle sources of faculty satisfactions and frustrations.
The generation gap has been an exaggerated condition of our time so
often described for us that we cannot be quite sure whether a true
condition is being described or the description is making us think the
condition exists. But our time aside, there is always a generation
gap. Few young people understand the old, and the old, who feel
that they don't understand the young, may feel guilty or vexed or
regretful because in some way they are failing to reach back to what
they once were.

There is no question that the young teacher, for all his
inexperience, has a marked advantage over his older colleagues.
Professing, a professorship, still has connotations of long years of
study removed from the ordinary ways of men. No wonder young
professors (even if they happen to be instructors or even graduate
assistants) arouse a certain awe among students not much younger
than they are. Youth more easily identifies with youth, speaks their
language, enters into the informal teaching relationships this age
seems very much to want. We need not deny these possibilities to
older teachers; it is enough to recognize that age may well mean a
moving away from an easy identification with students.

In what can be regarded as the normal course of faculty
development, at least for a part of the faculty, the professor as he
grows older finds more of his teaching taken up with graduate
students. On the face of it, the arrangement seems to follow out
some natural design. It uses the highest learning at the highest level
of instruction, the most experienced teachers with the most
advanced students, and matches the specialized professional interest
of the student with that of the master. But the separations all these
imply have not had a beneficent effect upon undergraduate learning

and only a peculiar (and not necessarily beneficial) effect upon graduate education. One could even argue that the acceptance of such natural drifts has created the gulfs between identifiable groups that this age is finding so hard to bridge.

For that reason as well as for reason of the older professor's well-being, we should do more than let the young teach the young. If we want more senior professors profitably engaged with undergraduate students, we need to increase the attractiveness of undergraduate teaching, not only in general ways, but in ways that correspond to the skills and preferences of individual professors. The freshman seminars at Stanford for example, have been successful probably because the seminar format may better suit the majority of senior professors and because it has allowed such professors to teach subjects in which they have a keen personal or professional interest. The idea is a transferable one to large numbers of institutions. The economics of mass instruction still might be served by identifying the really skillful lecturers among a senior staff and letting them teach courses to beginning students which would not fall into the traditional survey and introductory patterns. These would be popular lectures on important subjects and need exclude no subject matter except that which depended heavily on mastering of technical skill or knowledge. For a senior professor who has been encouraged to keep alive a range of teaching skills, it should not be impossible to bring even the specialized knowledge of a limited subject to a broad audience in ways that would encourage their general growth if not their specific competence.

As a last suggestion, much more could be done to establish contact between professors and students outside the classroom. It cannot be done by force, nor by Mickey Mouse social ploys, nor by well-intended exhortation. Invitations may need to be extended, accidental meetings "arranged," course loads relaxed, professional duties re-defined, in all the ingenious ways that students and faculty and administrators can devise. "While we teach knowledge," Erich Fromm writes, "we are losing that teaching which is the most important one for human development: the teaching which can only be given by the simple presence of a mature, loving person."

If it were possible to make student achievements more visible to faculty, that, too, might exercise a salutary influence. Departments have fairly little contact with their alumni. The lack is most noticeable with undergraduate alumni, not only because there are more of them to be kept track of, but because most graduating seniors lack the professional identification that graduate students have. A senior professor may opt for teaching graduate students because he gets to meet former students at professional meetings or sees their work in print or has his own work acknowledged in a former student's footnotes. With undergraduate teaching, few continuing evidences of a teacher's work make themselves known. Perhaps the best one can advocate is the duty of administrative structures to keep lines of communication between students and professors open, to provide opportunities for exchange, and to seek ways that the effects of teaching can be perceived.

Changing Conditions

One of the most difficult circumstances that senior professors may face is rapidly changed objectives within an institution, bringing with it differences in students, administrators, and instructional climate. The situation is a familiar one during the past period of growth. It is one we may be glad to see less often in a period of relative stability.

From one point of view — the college's future — the college is moving to higher goals, the progress toward which is impeded by the presence of faculty members not up to the demands of a higher level of excellence. From another viewpoint — the faculty members' — the college to which they gave so much now threatens to dislodge them. Few administrations have changed the character of a college without fearful strain, and many colleges in the past two decades have gone through such transformations. It is another aspect of the deadwood problem when large portions of a faculty become deadwood, not by the measures of competence which had been in effect when they joined the faculty but by new measures coming into being because of the changing objectives of a college.

Here again, "deadwood" obscures the specifics of the problem. It is certainly reasonable to expect an individual in any occupation to adapt to change. Failure to adapt in private employments makes itself apparent in the withdrawal of customers or clients or patients. Within an institutional framework, these immediate consequences may not reveal themselves very clearly to the individual professor. The first necessity in meeting the obsolescence of faculty in a changing college is informing the faculty early and continually of impending changes and the nature of such changes. Equally important is the presence of a governing structure that makes the faculty an important party to such changes. With such communication and with such faculty responsibility and power, the faculty itself can establish ways of assisting those faculty members who have difficulty in changing teaching objectives and methods, or in adapting to the general goals the institution is trying to achieve.

Such common sense suggestions gloss over the difficulties of effecting change, particularly in senior professors whose length of service and loyalty to an institution as it was arouse strong personal as well as professional resistance. Such faculty members cannot be merely steam-rollered by great numbers of ambitious young men, as I have observed happening on campuses moving rapidly from teachers college status to state universities. Nor should they merely be contained or cut off awaiting their retirement in five or six years. The problems change creates need confronting, not only institutionally, but individually. Left to themselves, the faculty member already aggrieved because the old ways cannot be preserved may become more aggrieved still. Well in advance of those changes which are inevitable, a chairman or dean, better still a body of the faculty charged with that responsibility, should counsel with those individuals most opposed to or hurt by change to see what can be done to keep teachers effectively operating in a new setting.

The Effects of Tenure

Tenure rightfully, I think, offers protection to the faculty member who would be arbitrarily displaced in a major shift within an institution. And tenure serves the profession well if it causes those within a changing college to act with restraint and consideration.

Unthinking attacks on tenure often single out "senile old professors" as proof of tenure's evil effects. Students are particularly given to making such condemnations. Yet, older professors can make the kind of impact on students that keeps them from being thought of as either old or tenured, much less senile. Nevertheless, tenure will probably continue to be identified, however unjustly, with the older professors who use it as protection against their infirmities.

As much as tenure is criticized in this respect, I think it is not the central issue. Tenure, itself, has little to do with why employers proceed cautiously against those individuals who seem to have come to a dead end some years short of retirement. If one has put in several decades of apparently satisfactory service with any employer, summary dismissal in his later years neither is nor should be possible. Academic institutions protect themselves in the same ways as other institutions. They shift the individual into less demanding positions, relieve him of crucial responsibilities, perhaps provide opportunity for early retirement. Retirement in the teaching profession, however, does not customarily come before 65. One of the recommendations of the Santa Fe Conference on the Teaching Environment was for extending the period in which full or partial retirement would be customary, respected, and possible. Some administrators have pointed out the possibility of using 62 as an early retirement date. The availability of social security payments would make it possible for an institution to raise an individual's total retirement pay to a level that would make such early retirement attractive. And the difference in salary between that of the senior professor and his young replacement would make it economically possible for the institution.

It is well to keep in mind that older professors can be asked to do too little as well as too much. This is particularly true of committee work and similar responsibilities. The growth in numbers in the lower and middle ranks of the faculty has increased the numbers of faculty members in these ranks holding responsible university positions. The growth and change characteristic of institutions in the past decade has probably inclined many institutions to draw upon the younger faculty. A failure to use the older faculty sufficiently or in important ways may, then, be suspected as a current cause of ineffectiveness among older faculty members. It is easy at any time for an administration to want fresh ideas, vigorous individuals on important committees. Older faculty members may be passed over both because they have served so often and because a younger man appears to be a better bet for a particular job. The mismanagement — the lack of management — in university committee selection is a source of much justified complaining on the part of a faculty. The drift is inevitably toward a few members of a faculty doing a large share of committee work. Conversely, the best way to have a career free of committee assignments is never to perform such an assignment well in the first place. But the older faculty member who followed that course to his complete satisfaction through mid-career may find it less satisfying in his older years. No one now pays attention to him; no one seems to respect him; no one wishes to draw upon his services. Committee work seems both inescapable and ill-regarded. The best way out, it seems to me, is to keep scrupulous track of committee assignments and to make use of all the faculty whatever their age and whatever their apparent interest and competence.

What Chairmen Might Do

Professor Helbling's experience as chairman of a large department led him to put down a number of things chairmen might do to preserve faculty effectiveness:

1. Seek out the area where the man showed genuine interest in the past; courses he created or proposed; work he did on his own initiative. Then take the risk of reviving those areas whether "needed" or not.

2. Do not overlook a man's professional avocations. They may furnish a clue to the manner in which his enthusiasm can be rekindled. General education, honors and other interdepartmental programs, perhaps even the "free university," may be able to incorporate successfully a man's unorthodox interests into their offerings — "unorthodox" in the sense of straddling existing departmental structures.

3. Using the same guide of interest, explore the possibility of encouraging productive and enthusiastic colleagues to collaborate on planning, on courses, and on projects and books.

4. Consult frequently with the man — not merely on routine or mechanical matters — but on his notions of the program, the interests of the students, the interests of the staff. Participation is the key to productive organizational interest and performance.

5. Do not force the man to do chores he obviously dislikes, or to teach courses he obviously has no enthusiasm for. If there are such chores to be done or courses which must be taught, then hire staff really interested in those aspects of the program or simply trim down the present program and restructure it.

I would like to add to these one suggestion to administrators:

Don't let the vexations that arise from the singular, troublesome cases magnify the deadwood problem.

A wise college president once told his faculty, "I spend ninety percent of my time explaining ten percent of you." The percentages may not be exact, but the situation is one any administrator can recognize. The wise response is not to let the visible evidences of human imperfection cloud one's vision everywhere. The commission to study tenure at the University of Utah tried to get some measure of the actual number of ineffective individuals on the faculty. The commission's questionnaire asked faculty respondents whether they personally believed that one or more members of their departmental staffs should be dismissed. Thirty percent of the respondents indicated such a belief. However, the commission pointed out, this raw figure should be carefully qualified. Many of these responses may have come from different members of a few departments. Responding faculty members also expected that some of those deserving dismissal would, in fact, leave or be dismissed, and that the continued employment of about *half* of those *not* dismissed would be due to factors other than tenure. In addition, the question did not attempt to identify any ages, and presumably the identified incompetents were spread throughout all age groups. With such allowances made, the number of certified deadwood among the older faculty might prove to be quite small. No figure can be set as to what number of poorly performing faculty and what degree of poor performance should be tolerated within a college or university faculty of a given size. But as generosity is generally favorable to teaching, so I think it might be regarded as generally favorable to meeting the deadwood problem.

It is mistaken generosity, I think, to give substance to the myth that once tenure and the full professorship are achieved, all evaluation of a professor's competence ceases. Student ratings probably do come as a shock to some senior professors both because they are unused to being judged and because lifelong habits are hard to break. But in my many discussions of evaluation, I have encountered just as stiff resistance from young professors as older ones. As a matter of fact, the two professors who wrote indignant letters of protest about student ratings — one threatening to resign from the AAUP; the other to have the AAUP remove me from my position — were presumably younger faculty members, one an assistant, the other an associate professor. I see no good reason for excluding senior professors from student evaluations. Nor have I noticed any strong manifestation of interest in such an exclusion, either from students or from senior professors themselves.

There are good reasons however, for not keeping senior professors under the same kind or frequency of review as faculty members during their probationary period. Presumably, a full professor has established his competence. Performance is another matter, and institutional practices should be such that a department chairman or dean does not completely lose touch with how senior professors carry out their responsibilities. Besides, the senior professor probably benefits from continuing to have his work — teaching and scholarship — noticed. There is much to be gained, therefore, from continuing with some kind of periodic formal review of the senior professors.

The worst problems of diminished effectiveness are those which involve the faculty member who hangs on because letting go is letting go of life itself. In any administrator's experience are instances in which age has created or intensified such anguishing personal problems. Such instances defy solution, and compassion may be the principal resource those involved in such problems can draw upon.

Fortunately, these effects of aging are the exception rather than the rule. The concluding remarks are directed to all those who sometimes feel they are or might be becoming some garden variety of deadwood, that is, to most members of the faculty over thirty:

- *Don't nurse grievances in silence. Though the stress in this chapter has been upon assisting the individual on maintaining effectiveness, the individual has a responsibility, too, for making his complaints, needs, frustrations known.*

- *Don't be satisfied with the easy explanations for an apparent decline of effectiveness as a teacher. The students may not be that different or wrong; the administration may not be that insensitive; the conditions may not be that bad.*

- *Don't let what you have done or have been doing keep you from seeking out other things that might still be done.*

- *Don't permit yourself to be set aside as past making a contribution to the common good.*

- *Don't fail to ask for recognition of facts of health and aging in working out professional responsibilities.*

- *Don't despair. The university, despite its fragmentation, is a community and the well-being of its members is the concern of all.*

6. The Reward System

The college and university reward system is commonly blamed for the neglect of teaching. The AAUP Committee on College and University Teaching wrote in its report of 1933: "It is idle to profess any special solicitude for the good teacher when existing conditions are such that a man's success in research is everywhere rewarded as a matter of course, while success in teaching is not." Elsewhere, however, the report was careful not to pit research against teaching, and its criticism of the reward system, though prominent, does not seem to be as emphatic as I have heard expressed by faculty members today.

Logan Wilson, writing in 1942, said: "Indeed it is no exaggeration to say that the most critical problem confronted in the social organization of any university is the proper evaluation of faculty services, and giving due recognition through the impartial assignment of status." John Gustad's surveys of policies and practices in faculty evaluation in 1961 provide a data basic for describing the reward system as it existed then. Gustad's summary of findings begins: "The majority of institutions studied said they placed principal weight on teaching ability, but no even approximately effective method of evaluating this seems to be in use. Scholarship is evaluated by bulk rather than quality. Other factors are evaluated on a hit-or-miss basis." A similar survey conducted by Astin and Lee for the American Council on Education in 1966 did not differ markedly from Gustad's. The Astin and Lee report concluded:

> The uniformly high importance assigned to class-room teaching by some 1,110 deans in junior colleges, teachers colleges, liberal arts colleges, and universities could be interpreted to mean that the so-called neglect of undergraduate teaching is more a myth than a reality.

However, in the light of the data about how teaching effectiveness is actually evaluated, the apparent over-all importance assigned to classroom teaching is not as reassuring as it first appears to be. Citing classroom teaching as a major factor in personnel decisions does not encourage improved teaching as long as teaching ability is more likely to be evaluated on the basis of scholarly research and publication rather than information more directly relevant to effective performance in the classroom. It is clear from this survey that deans and chairmen are overwhelmingly important as the source of information about teaching effectiveness. If they wish to strike a balance between classroom teaching and scholarly research and publication, they must find ways to avoid using the latter to prove the former.

The reward system described in the two surveys shows many institutional variations, but these common elements can be discerned:

The initiative for promotion, tenure, and salary increases usually comes from the chairman of a department.

Within the department, a committee, often of senior professors, less often of the department as a whole, may have a role in discussing and shaping the recommendations.

Recommendations go to the dean, who has the responsibility for reviewing, supporting, or not supporting the recommendation, and forwarding on.

A college- or university-wide committee on rank and tenure may have an important part in the higher level review process.

Final decision is usually made by a higher academic officer, either the academic vice-president or president, usually in consultation with the dean. Approval of the trustees is usually pro forma.

Gustad makes a number of important observations about the workings of this system: substantial knowledge of performance is heavily dependent on the chairman's and/or department's recommendation; chairmen and deans are crucial; and there is an internal conflict between attachment to the informal and imprecise procedures which prevail and the need for more objective and precise measures. The large and favorable response to this project's booklet, *The Recognition and Evaluation of Teaching,* may indicate that the profession is willing to resolve the latter conflict in favor of more carefully defined policies and procedures. The discussion in the booklet suggests, "that the majority of vexing disputes between faculty members and department chairmen or other officers of administration occur because of failure to clarify what is expected of a faculty member, to set forth the criteria for retention and advancement, or to communicate clearly decisions or judgments of an individual's competence and the basis for such decisions or judgments."

Against this background, it seems reasonable to say that if the reward system is to change in ways more favorable to teaching, criteria for advancement must be more precisely defined, judgments on performance more broadly based, and an avowed intention to reward teaching carried out in practice. Procedures for advancement will probably become more formal, and policies will have to be set forth more openly and in greater detail. In addition, attitude changes will need to take place within the profession, particularly in the graduate schools, the departments, and the professional disciplines which support both.

Defining Criteria for Advancement

There is no great argument within the profession about the broad responsibilities of a faculty member. Scholarship, teaching, and service are accepted almost everywhere as the major ones. In the community colleges, teaching and service, particularly services involving students, are emphasized to the exclusion of research. In the universities, scholarship is given great weight, professional services are important, and teaching, while emphasized in policies seems neglected in practice. The importance accorded each shifts from department to department and with an individual institution's growth and aspirations. The past two decades have emphasized the development of research and graduate work, although the growth of the community colleges has created a large segment of the academic community in which research accomplishments receive little emphasis. The reward systems in all institutions, however, is affected by the common training that students receive who go on to advanced degrees. Here, scholarship looms large, and the fact that an institutional reward system is importantly shaped by the faculty may account for the weighting scholarship, teaching, and service receive in all institutions.

There is some chance that the reward system would better fit the individual college or university if criteria for advancement were set forth in detail and frequently reviewed. For it is in the statement of criteria at a school-wide level that the generality creeps in which seems to support good but unfulfilled intentions. It is one thing to say that "research is expected of all ranks;" it is another to say "two published articles in reputable national journals are required for promotion to assistant professor." It is one thing to say "excellent teaching is expected of all faculty members" and another to say "evidence of consistent excellence in teaching shall be based upon evaluation by students, first-hand observation by colleagues, and careful review of class materials and student achievements."

Faculties are hesitant to specify the details of satisfactory performance of responsibilities that must fit a large number of individuals. Yet, it is only by specifying that an institution can recognize individual differences among faculty, can make the most of the diverse talents, and can reward them fairly. Operating under criteria that will fit everyone, gain the concurrence of everyone, an institution is fated to hold up the highest and vaguest of aspirations. The faculty members are fated to enjoy, if they can, the illusion of meeting such high standards, while fretting under unfair demands, inequities of treatment, and failure to recognize specific worth. In the large universities, as university-wide rank and salary committees find out, the supposed uniformity of policies breaks down each time a set of recommendations comes in.

At the university-wide level, the statement of general policies may always escape exact formulation. But that is not the place for precise statements of practice, anyway. At best, the college or university can take the faculty into its confidence and periodically state where its values lie. If the institution's aspirations as a research center cause faculty talent and funds to be concentrated in graduate work, it should try to make that clear. If undergraduate teaching is to get the major share of attention, then the possible effects upon faculty members primarily interested in research should be pointed out. It is hard for such statements to come out of a college or university, for the institution, like the faculty member, would like to be virtuous in all ways. The desire is inescapable, for to some degree, research and teaching and service are unitary activities, even more for an institution than for an individual faculty member.

Nevertheless, a faculty should ask for such clarifications of intentions, and prominent members of the administration should get into discourse with faculty and students to give further clarification to written statements. At the very least, prospective faculty members should not be deceived into thinking an institution is what it is not. If the institution itself does not honestly and candidly appraise and describe its aims, department chairmen are not likely to give new faculty members an accurate assessment of what is expected of them.

Defining Goals in Financial Terms

What the college or university might provide, rather than an eloquent statement of current goals from the president's office, is an accounting sheet from the treasurer's office showing where money has in fact been spent and where it is proposed to be spent in the future. In the long, slow gains in faculty involvement in university governance, least gains have been made in having some share in or even knowledge of overall budget allocations. For though financial figures can be misleading, they can also disclose many things which otherwise might be obscure. Understanding the actual costs of graduate work as against undergraduate instruction has already had an impact upon higher education committees in state legislatures, for example. Breakdowns of administrative and equipment costs chargeable to instruction and to research would be instructive. A salary breakdown in terms of teaching loads and research productivity would furnish useful data. Perhaps exact and open financial accounting is the only way institutions might be brought to recognize where their priorities are rather than where they are professed to be.

Department Responsibilities

Given specific policy guidance, departments could go very far toward developing specific criteria for advancement. The assurance a department needs is that its carrying out of university policies will not result in unfavorable treatment. The insistence upon such assurance may force the university to make distinctions it would otherwise not make. Specifically, that research is more of an expectation in one department than another; that certain kinds of teaching in certain kinds of departments are of less value than other kinds in other places; that a high standard of excellence is expected in the performance of all tasks but that some tasks are worth more than others. All of these are evident in practice, but they seldom appear in statements of policy.

The department's task is also one of recognizing the department's various aims and the ways faculty members can best be encouraged to carry them out. Again, what one faculty member does to earn full rewards may not be the same as another, though a similar degree of competence should be expected of each. Specification is the only way to do this well. The question is not that the department values excellent teaching, but what precise value does it place upon it? Enough to forgive a man for not publishing a book? Enough to justify his continued involvement with students to the exclusion of committee work? Enough to gather the kind of evidence which will justify an early promotion? None of the questions which come to mind is easy to answer. Some may not submit to precise answers. But only by discussing criteria at this degree of specification will it be possible to arrive at criteria which are fair to individual faculty members and effective in carrying out departmental aims.

In general, departments in the humanities are more resistant to such specification than those in the sciences. A college of engineering I visited this past year had arrived at a promotional point system. All the tasks a member of the faculty could be expected to perform had been assigned weighted values, and within each of these values, points were assigned for quality of performance. The faculty member knew how many total points must be earned for various kinds of advancement, and he could set about piling up his points to achieve the ends he desired. Many faculty members express dismay over such a mechanical system. The committees on career development have advised caution in using quantitative measures. For the use of figures does not solve the problem of defining values, and it may lead to placing an excessive valuation on those things which can be quantified. Specification is possible short of quantification, and a department can hardly claim to have a defensible reward system unless it has detailed, written specification of criteria for advancement.

Written specification, however, should not preclude periodic, open discussions of the value, applicability, and effectiveness of the criteria. A yearly review is not inappropriate, and as changes take place both within institutions and the profession at large, more strenuous discussions may be advisable. Young professors are now entering the profession with other aims than carrying out conventional statements of teaching or research or service responsibilities. Departments could use such opportunities to review their total objectives as well as the criteria for individual advancement. Equally important, such open reviews add to the possibility (never 100 per cent) that all faculty members will understand the reward structure, be in general harmony with it, and feel it is assisting them in their own self-fulfillment as teachers.

I would suggest one addition to the general criteria used which might help resolve the conflicts between teaching and research. It might also assist in adding a useful supporting measure of both teaching and research activities. The fact that research is chiefly measured by publication does much to explain the existence of "publish or perish." Nevertheless, activities instead of research, such as performance in the arts or musical composition, have gained general acceptance. "Scholarship" is a somewhat broader term for "research" as "publication" is a narrower one. "Scholarship and creative work" would be an even broader category. One department includes among its criteria for judging faculty competence, "superior intellectual attainment, including scholarship, motivation, the capacity for growth, and other intangible qualities." This is an attempt to define the presence of an active, inquiring, interesting mind employing itself in the service of teaching and research (and for that matter, in service as well). Inclusion of such a criterion should not be an excuse to find virtue where none, otherwise, would exist. Insisting upon tangible evidences of such qualities would be the best way of resisting such a tendency. Moreover, it might be a way of dropping "research" as the single standard to which all activities outside the classroom relate. Formal research might become a sub-category under such a heading as "Scholarship and Creative Work," just as certain kinds of teaching might become sub-categories under "Teaching," and published work a sub-category under the appropriate major responsibility.

Broadening The Base For Judgment

Even when criteria are carefully defined and set forth, the problem remains of judging how well the faculty member has performed specified tasks. Qualitative judgments cannot be set aside, though the difficulty of making them is greater than specifying and even weighting kinds of services. The best possibility of reaching reasonably accurate qualitative judgments is to base them on data from a number of different kinds of measures. Research, particularly in those universities which emphasize it, is subject to qualitative measures in asking for outside opinions, by considering the editorial standards of the place of publication, or by the actual reading of such work by the faculty. More accurate data and a broader base for judging teaching can be achieved by using both student and colleague judgments based upon various measures of teaching effectiveness and by seeking more accurate evidences of the faculty member's effect upon student achievements. Expectations as to quality of performance should be set forth in as precise terms as possible and with specific indications as to what measures of quality are to be used.

The discussion thus far has been confined to university or department criteria for faculty performance. The department's responsibility for framing specific criteria adds to the power the department already has in being the locus for first-hand judgment as to performance. Thus, though it is necessary to have a department's values reflected in printed criteria, it still may not be sufficient to keep a department from maintaining a restricted view of its own purposes and those of higher education. When you add the tight linkage between departments and professional disciplines, the possibilities of a narrowed point of view are greater still. Though, as has been mentioned, outside judgment of published work may be a way of asserting qualitative judgments, larger questions of quality may escape attention. An eighteenth century literary scholar, for example, is likely to have his published work judged by other eighteenth century scholars. Some sense of its worth within eighteenth century scholarship may emerge, but very little light is ever shed on the value of eighteenth century scholarship. Trivial scholarship exists in abundance within the university because of the multitude of research specialities protective in terms of internal evaluations and seldom subject to any external measures of worth. The universities have no mechanisms at all for seeing research in terms of an overarching set of values. There is even very little in the way of overarching values to hold up for any of the services performed by professors operating within and being judged by members of a department.

Second, student input, preferably as an independent part of a recommendation, should be insisted upon. The acceptance of student evaluation is growing, but faculty are not aware that getting student input is the institution's responsibility as well as the students'. If student evaluation is to be regarded as an intrinsic part of judging faculty competence, faculty will probably have to assist in seeing that it is well done. If faculty, students, and administrators can agree upon procedures for obtaining reliable input, then I think such input should go directly to the dean's office, and be judged equally with the department's input as the measure of a professor's performance as a teacher.

Third, various other measures of teaching effectiveness can be sought. Sampling alumni, exit interviews with senior majors, measures of students' accomplishments, self-evaluation, and visiting of classes are the most obvious ones.

But with all of these, the greater part of data will come through the department and be restricted in some of the same ways as the views of departmental colleagues. One way of getting beyond this restriction would be to establish a university-wide teaching committee to undertake first-hand observations of teachers in action, either by actual visiting or by using video tape. The observations need not even have a direct connection with promotion procedures. It is conceivable that if (1) the work of such a committee were recognized as intended for faculty development, and (2) observation of teaching performance were an on-going responsibility instead of a once-a-year review, then some exposure of teachers to discerning colleagues outside of their departments would be possible. Given sufficient time over a number of years to observe faculty members as teachers, such a committee might provide a very valuable kind of data.

Carrying Out Intentions

The most difficult problem of the reward system is that of carrying out intentions. If a university actually had the nerve to fire a half-dozen or so of its worst teachers, I have been told, the reward system would begin to take on meaning. Or conversely, if it took excellent young teachers who had published little or nothing and elevated them to full professors that would help. Neither, I think, would achieve as much as its advocates believe. I think the best bet lies with the less spectacular way of department chairmen and deans working hard to see that policies square with practices. I single out these individuals because together they have the power to do it, and both have the means of letting the academic community know what has been done. It is also, as a matter of fact, what individuals in administrative positions are supposed to do.

Department chairmen, even in very democratic departments, have a great deal of power. In fact, they may have greater power if they have come into the position by the democratic mandate of the department. For by such a process, a department indicates in advance its trust of the person. The nature of the office is that it exists to do many things the individual faculty member doesn't want to do. Initiative counts for a great deal in academic politics, and the chairman, as regards advancement procedures, has full use of this power. If data on teaching effectiveness are going to be gathered and used by the department, the chairman will probably be responsible for doing it. With or without supporting data, the chairman's comments on a faculty member's teaching are often conclusive. This does not say that department chairmen will come forward to see that excellent teaching receives its proper reward. But if the criteria have been set forth, if the institution's support has been unequivocally stated, responsibility is fixed upon the department head for putting policies into practice.

Deans have both a prominent part in appointing chairmen and in being the first level of review of rank and salary recommendations. They also have a chance of seeing teaching in its broader practices and its consequence for a college. Exhorting deans to act responsibly is one possibility. Suggesting a mechanism whereby their judgment might be more effectively applied may be a better one. Michael Scriven of the University of California at Berkeley has suggested that recommendations from the department to the dean come in the form of specific recommendations, with supporting evidence, on each of the agreed-upon broad criteria for advancement. That is, the chairman would not recommend a person's promotion based upon a total assessment of his various strengths, but would make only separate recommendations on his performance as teacher, scholar, committee member and the like. The dean would then have the task, in consultation with or apart from the department chairman, of assessing the total strengths and weaknesses and arriving at the judgment of the person's whole performance.

The merits of such a plan are that it whittles away at the almost exclusive power of the department both to gather evidence and to make judgment. With someone else making judgment, the department would probably be more zealous in gathering evidence and the evidence might be less compromised by the personal feelings that enter into the judgments of colleagues. Such a procedure does not, however, eliminate the possibility that the dean might choose to disregard evidence or weight it according to his own sense of values. While it increases both the tension and the need for trust between deans and departments, it does seem to broaden the actual basis for judgment. If in such a process, a committee on rank and salary had the specific charge of reviewing the dean's recommendation, and an aggrieved department or individual had a chance to be heard there, some real gains in squaring policy with practice might result.

Feedback on the Workings of the Reward System

From the outside, the reward system in higher education is seen in terms of its more visible results. One notably poor teacher who happens to be a highly productive and specialized scholar seems to be cause enough for singling out the university's disdain for teaching. One unpublished assistant professor who is being let go for what may be good reasons is sufficient to provoke strong words about the publish-or-perish philosophy. Students in a number of universities have taken up the cause of popular young professors who are being dismissed seemingly in disregard of their ability as teachers. In such instances, the concern for justice in the individual case is mixed with a strongly felt response to the apparent workings of a hostile reward system. Little enough can be done about getting individuals to act objectively on the basis of full instead of partial evidence, but much could be done to inform the academic community about the positive ways in which the reward system works.

The whole process, I think, has been too shrouded in secrecy. The faculty member up for review seldom has the opportunity to be heard before the decision is reached and is given a generalized account, if he is informed at all, of the basis for the decision after the fact. Outside the department, very little is known about the department's deliberations, though conscientious administrators try to set standards for fairness and adequacy of procedures. There may be little that can be done to make practices more open without destroying the confidentiality which the individual may rightly insist upon. But, the department chairman and dean do have opportunities to give useful information to the academic community. As simple a matter as calling attention to the accomplishments — in teaching, research, service — of those being promoted would counteract the tendency to have only grievances gain attention. The formality of letting the faculty member himself know in writing the basis for a department's judgment is a way of eliminating rumor and grievance at an important source. Students can be drawn into discussions of the full dimensions of department judgments and be asked to respond to department policies and practices in regard to advancement. An honest response to student questions about an individual professor may add to general understanding of how the reward system works and forestall students' making a cause out of a specific instance.

Appointments of Distinguished Teachers

The reward system as it affects teachers will probably continue to seem to reward the more visible aspects of professorial competence. That is why an institutional reward system might seek to give some room to academic advancement outside of departmental structures. It should be possible to maintain a number of positions of a university nature, for which the chief requirement would be superiority as a teacher and the route to which would be outside ordinary channels. The effect would be to create a visible and functioning position which both rewarded teaching and attested to the university's support of it. Such a procedure would meet one aspect of the general hostility to teaching awards: that the one-shot cash gift is little as compared with regular advancement for excellent teaching. The other objection is not met and is a matter needing careful consideration. That is the means by which either awards for distinguished teachers or appointments of distinguished teachers would be made. Very diverse methods exist for naming the winners of teaching awards. Most are weakened by being insufficiently understood by the faculty. Many are inadequate in terms of nominating procedures, selection criteria, screening, and final choice. Teaching positions outside of the departmental framework would need to be made with even greater care. It does not, however, seem impossible to establish policies and procedures which would be acceptable to the university community. The active presence of such teachers specifically for the enhancement of instruction is an important way of both recognizing and rewarding superior teaching.

Changing Attitudes

Changing the reward system is not only a matter of improving institutional practices in advancing faculty members through the ranks. At the heart of the matter may be changing attitudes which are somewhat vaguely ascribed to "professors" or "the profession" but which are nevertheless strongly felt by individuals and embedded in the reward system. One is the placing of teaching below scholarship. Another is prizing specialized competence over general learning. Another is measuring the worth of teaching by the general level at which it is practiced. Another is basing a professor's worth on the formal credentials he must possess. Others have been mentioned in the course of this discussion. Such attitudes are not uniformly held nor reacted against.

How to change such attitudes is the difficult question. Allan Cartter locates the source of current attitudes toward research and teaching in the graduate schools. The upheavals within almost all the professional disciplines suggest that there are entrenched attitudes there which some part of the current generation of graduate students wants to see displaced. Conventionally, the young are pointed out as being most accessible to attitude changes. Clearly, the graduate schools and the scholarly disciplines have great responsibility for the impressions both make upon the young scholar at the beginning of his or her career. But the problem, like all problems of reforming human beings, has no handle or too many handles. At times, it all seems to come down to saying that if college professors would only recognize the importance of teaching, give it the full measure of their devotion, a shift in the reward system would follow.

Lest this chapter end with such a pious hope, here are a number of concrete suggestions that may lead to changes in attitudes:

Increasing recognition of teaching outside the salary and rank structure. Students can be a powerful force here; a diminishing of zeal for rating teachers might be channeled into broad concern for teaching and learning.

Appointing distinguished teachers to positions which lie outside the departmental structure.

Increasing the ways to use excellent teachers. Institutional hospitality to new teaching/learning environments is important, as is outside support of excellent teachers as visitors to other campuses and as catalysts for increased recognition of teaching.

Examining leaves and grants to increase the possibilities that teachers will find them helpful in specific ways and at crucial stages in their careers.

Convincing graduate schools and professional disciplines that they need to give as much attention to development of teachers as of scholars.

Questioning the assumption that only competitive measures will work in improving the reward system. Removing competitive pressures may be a means for some teachers in some places to make teaching flower.

Exploring ways of examining and rewarding whole departments for excellence in teaching.

7. Special Considerations

Throughout this booklet, a necessary assumption has been that the development of effective college teachers can be discussed in ways that apply to many teachers and many institutions. The makeup of the various career development conferences extended the project's reach to members of the academic community from different disciplines and kinds of colleges and of different ages, backgrounds, and positions. The project could probably have learned much from holding separate conferences for various groups, but limited resources made that impossible. While there was great diversity of opinion in conference discussions, both formal and informal talk seemed to emphasize the common experience that those in higher educational institutions share.

Obviously, the observations and recommendations made here cannot apply to all teachers and places. Specific needs vary in time as well as in place for individuals and institutions. And one cannot do much more than suggest the differences within institutions which affect individual faculty members' development. This chapter will look briefly at some of the important differences which may affect the college teacher's career in the sciences, humanities, and the fine arts. It will also examine teaching and career development in the community colleges, the predominantly Negro colleges, and with respect to women within the profession.

Differences Between Disciplines

There is no question that policies and practices with respect to faculty development are complicated by the differing aims and values of members of the university community. Faculty members within a department do not often see much beyond the practices and assumptions of that department. Reward systems which try to extend fair treatment across all departments run into such specific problems as the rapid advancement to full professor expected in the law school, the prominence given to team research in some of the sciences, the inapplicability of research in the performing arts, and the pride in community service in colleges of agriculture or of social work. Such examples only suggest the multitude of differences which affect attitudes toward teaching.

Research studies and casual observation both reveal that the disciplines vary widely in the proportion of graduate students who go on to college and university teaching. The percentages vary somewhat from year to year, but in general the sciences and social sciences offer many more job opportunities outside teaching than the humanities. A research career outside the university is a real option for chemists, physicists, psychologists, economists, and engineers, for over half of those who receive Ph.D. degrees in these disciplines do not go into university positions. In English, languages, history, philosophy, and political science almost all of those with Ph.D. degrees become college or university professors.

Unfortunately, the same universities and the same Ph.D. programs provide graduate study for all of these. Ann Heiss notes that for students in the humanities, "teaching and reflective writing are the expressive forms of scholarship." In the physical and biological sciences, "students who elect these fields tend to be attracted to research and view it as a major activity in their future careers." "The social sciences," she adds, "face more complicated problems in providing research preparation." If one adds the large amounts of outside money that have come into the university for support of research in the last decade, he can begin to appreciate the force of the research emphasis upon all those electing an academic career.

I have written at length elsewhere about these crucial differences, and I will quote a concluding paragraph from one of these discussions:

> Specialization and research as the universities now define them are not necessarily the highest attainments for the humanist. Knowledge which concerns itself with people and their ideas must be broad and it must be humane. But the feeling persists that if the humanities could be as exact, as receptive to technology, as efficient, as pure, as science, they would somehow strike closer to the truth and reap the rewards society now denies them. In

some ways, the specialization in humanistic studies has been profitable. It has sharpened the humanists' critical insight; it has made scholarship more exacting; it has brought tools and techniques into the service of humanistic learning. On the other hand it has encouraged the collection of facts, the assembling of data, without regard for the value of the subject or of the work involved in pursuing it. It has demanded an intensity of focus which too often kills the tissue of thought. It has ingrained patterns of routine investigation which keep the young scholar from thinking large and the seasoned scholar from encouraging him to do so.

But it is not the wider effects I want to dwell on here. It is rather the need to acknowledge these differences of outlook as they affect policies and practices within the university and to work against those which seem to stand in the way of education. "The weakness in most Ph.D. programs," Ann Heiss has written, "seems to center on the fact that while the program professes to *educate* for research, in reality it *trains* for it." At the center of any effective career development system must be the attempt to foster both research and teaching which concern themselves with education, not mere training.

Some of the questions I see as most important in these matters are:

- *How can the specific demands and opportunities within individual disciplines be communicated to prospective college teachers?*

- *How can college teaching avoid the worst effects of being a second or third choice profession, a refuge for the chemist, physicist, writer, historian, artist, who cannot find other employment outside?*

- *How can college- or university-wide standards of excellence be maintained amidst different kinds of expectations from department to department?*

- *How can colleges or universities maintain common values while recognizing the different values that may be held within different disciplines?*

- *How can a plurality of views be maintained with respect to the nature of knowledge and its uses?*

The position of fine arts within the university will further define the basic question of differences among disciplines. The fine arts may be the only place within the university where formal research is not regarded as a prime obligation. Even then, the various departments in the fine arts have their internal divisions into the practitioners — those most concerned with studio courses — and the academicians — the art and music historians, aestheticians, educators and theoreticians. Other departments, of course, are not free from these distinctions, but I do not think there is anywhere else in the college or university structure where the practitioner plays such an important part in undergraduate education.

It is useful, therefore, to give some special consideration in a career development program to those who are directly involved in creative pursuits as contrasted with the academically oriented faculty. Lee Anne Miller, a member of the San Francisco conference group and a painter at the University of Missouri in Kansas City, raised two specific questions about how this booklet's general discussion might not apply to those in the fine arts:

> I think that the problem of inadequate training and consideration of teaching skills as part of the individual's educational process in graduate schools is a problem which cuts across all fields. But I sometimes wonder whether the various aspects of the problem are more intensified among the creative artists whose goal, time, and abilities may be so closely tied to the making of a particular end product that the individual's future dual role of teacher as well as artist is not even acknowledged. Therefore, the communicative skills, the philosophy and understanding of teaching tools, and the common elements of the teaching process which extend beyond the particulars of subject matter craft and knowledge may remain completely peripheral to the education of the potential teacher in the fine arts.
>
> It seems to me that there is perhaps a more integral identification of the person as teacher with the person as creator. Because of this entwinement, matters such as the deadwood problem take on additional nuances and complications. The person whose own work has become passé or who has ceased to create receives less respect as a conveyor of instruction. I think it would be easier for an academician whose research has dwindled to continue to gain respect as an authority within a particular subject matter discipline. It seems that there is usually a carryover

disintegration of the teaching effectiveness if the creative person's own interests and productivity have tapered off or declined badly in quality.

In my visits to classes on many campuses, I have been struck by the differences in teaching a studio course in the arts and in almost every other kind of teaching. There may be some analogies between laboratory courses in the sciences or tutorials within a range of disciplines or any courses which attempt to convey techniques or skills. But there is a crucial difference in all of these in the importance students attach to the teacher's own competence as a painter, or writer, or performer. It has taken strong efforts over the years to get such a traditional discipline as English to admit poets and novelists to department staffs somewhat on an equal plane of respect and practice as academically trained specialists. And English departments which permit creative work for the Ph.D. degree are still in the minority.

It is not to the point here to argue the question of how best to train artists. It may be, as many artists on university staffs argue, that the university and the graduate school are death to creativity. On the other hand, there is little question that universities afford associations, surroundings, and prospective employment which may be useful for those planning to be artists. But the question here is that the fine arts and increasingly the performing arts have a firm place in college and university structures, that many, many students choose courses in artistic fields, and that college and university faculty members teach them. The environment in which such faculty members engage in the dual career of teacher and artist must be as congenial as for the teacher and scholar.

We have not much more than scratched the surface of a complex subject. The most important generalization that might be made is to call for all disciplines to examine the relationships between teaching and the other career objectives that members of that discipline pursue. The creative artist's position has its singularities, but it shares with all disciplines a plurality of interests and/or obligations which makes it sometimes seem that teaching is not the primary interest of any faculty member in any discipline.

Community Colleges

Included in my visits to colleges during the past two years were visits to a half-dozen community colleges. In addition, I attended a number of meetings of junior college personnel and prior to the project worked closely with the Modern Language Association's study of English in the two-year college. The project has engaged in a good deal of correspondence with community college faculty members and administrators, and has surveyed the growing body of literature about the community college.

The position of most community colleges, somewhere between the public schools and the four-year colleges and universities, significantly affects faculty development. An uneasiness shows itself in the distress many community college faculty members feel toward the name "junior" college, even though the major professional association is called "the American Association of Junior Colleges." More important, the somewhat unsettled position of the community colleges affects appointments, advancement, and internal working conditions within them.

Some Characteristics of the Junior College Faculty

There is no need to go over the division between subject matter departments and schools of education, but such divisions as exist there also exist within the faculty of a community college. It is a safe generalization to say that most junior colleges draw heavily upon the public schools for both faculty and administrators. Faculties are younger than college and university faculties and the M.A. or M.A.T. is the most common faculty degree. Women comprise a larger percentage of the faculty; for example, 44 percent of the community college English faculty are women, roughly twice the percentage in four-year college departments. Teaching is clearly the chief responsibility of community college members, with average teaching loads running from 12 to 15 hours. Satisfactory teaching experiences and a demonstrated concern for the student are prime qualifications for new faculty members, and satisfactory teaching is much more the criterion for promotion and tenure than length of service, professional activity, and research. Departments within the community colleges have less autonomy than elsewhere in higher education, and faculties as a body have less of a part in university governance. Merit pay is an issue within the junior colleges, and most colleges probably operate on fixed salary scales similar to those in the public schools. Finally, innovations in teaching, particularly those which employ teaching/ learning equipment, are probably more actively pursued than in the college and university.

Spelling out these differences may slight the high degree of common interests and practices which tie the community colleges firmly to post high-school education. To the point here are the differences which might affect career development.

Many community college faculty members come into the community college from public school teaching. Those who come directly to the community college from graduate school usually come with a master's degree, and are less inclined to pursue the Ph.D. than those remaining in the graduate school. With some growth in graduate programs specifically aimed at junior college teaching, with beginning salaries better than competitive with other parts of higher education, the prospects of community college teaching are likely to remain attractive both to experienced public school teachers and to those just out of graduate school.

The debate about the appropriateness of the Doctor of Arts degree for junior college teaching, and the availability of more Ph.D.'s for junior college positions may make some changes, but overall, it seems to me, the junior college faculty is not likely to be overtrained or to be dominated by either public school or graduate school attitudes. **The implication for career development is that the community college will be a good place to support innovations in teaching and to build a highly effective teaching faculty.**

Needs and Limitations

A number of specific needs, however, arise in connection with attempts to institute career development systems. There is less leadership in the faculty and perhaps less understanding of the faculty position within the administration of the community college. Though the students come first, there is probably less activism among the community college students and a good deal more paternalism among both the administration and faculty. **Thus, a prime need is to develop faculty leadership that will work actively within the faculty for teaching and learning and move into administrative positions without losing sight of the teacher's needs.** Otherwise, community college work may take on some of the unfavorable aspects of teaching in the public school: administration and teachers sharply divided by marked differences in authority and salaries; severe limitations on advancement except by moving into administration; and teaching encumbered and restricted by central-ized control at the top. Faculty leadership is one of the ways that community colleges may resist some of the limitations placed on both teachers and teaching.

Chief among these limitations are those imposed by heavy teaching loads, large numbers of students, and restrictions on the curriculum. The MLA Junior College English Study observed that "despite a noticeable movement toward the twelve-hour load on many campuses, junior college English departments will not soon reach the nine-hour weekly teaching load proposed by the National Junior College Committee of CCCC in April, 1968." The problem is a complex one, for as junior colleges move to an identification with colleges and universities, teaching loads suffer by comparison. One of the problems the AAUP faced in arriving at a "workload statement" acceptable to the profession at large was to reconcile the heavy teaching loads in the community colleges (15 hours and above) with loads elsewhere in higher education (12 hours and below). The general assumption that superior teaching takes no more time than mediocre teaching operates as a deterrent to community college teachers whose only defense against too many classes and too many students is to do less for each. Since many community colleges have evening classes, many teachers are teaching over 15 hours, too much teaching under any arrangement.

A common means of justifying a heavy teaching load is to give the teacher two or more sections of the same class. The supposed savings in preparation time is somewhat illusory; whatever benefits are gained in reducing time involved are probably lost in the increased sameness of presentation, assignments, grading, and class-room activities. The AAUP statement recommends a maximum of 12 hours of undergraduate instruction with no more than six separate course preparations during the year. In the community colleges, heavy loads and a limited variety of teaching are a serious drawback to the kinds of teachers most inclined to expand the range of their competence. For counseling and working directly with students are strongly expected of community college faculty, and there is some evidence that these responsibilities get slighted when numbers of students and teaching loads are large. Allowance for professional growth, often maintained for college and university teachers in the form of time and support given to research, are hardly to be found in the community colleges. **Thus, the very thing that junior colleges are dedicated to — teaching — may suffer because too much of the same kind of teaching on the part of faculty members stands in the way of professional growth.**

One partial answer to these related problems is to somewhat free the curriculum from its ties with the four-year college and university. The junior college classrooms I have visited impressed me with the interchange between faculty and student and the willingness to depart from traditional modes of instructions. In some ways such flexibility was forced out of faculty members as a defense against the limited curriculum they must work within. As colleges and universities loosen their own curriculum structures, the junior colleges may experience a healthy opening up of theirs. Even in California's well-developed junior college system, terminal two-year students still comprise a substantial part of the graduates. Yet, outside vocational programs, the junior colleges must offer only those courses which match the first two year offerings in the state colleges. Though faculties generally have an irresistible urge to create more courses, the mood of junior college teachers seems to be toward more meaningful courses rather than toward adding courses as such. The increasing use of community service short courses at some schools has been both a way of serving community needs and of adding variety to the teaching assignment. The junior college might be an excellent place to experiment with a deliberately changing, *ad hoc,* curriculum, thus affording the faculty opportunity for greater variety within the limited two-year program.

Students in the Junior College

The final observation I will make is about the students in the community colleges. It is not precisely accurate to call the junior colleges "open-door colleges," though it is certainly true that they take a wider range of students than many four-year colleges or universities. In the MLA survey of junior colleges, only 72 percent considered themselves as open-door colleges which did not require an entrance examination. Nevertheless, the community college has become the place where a good deal of the teacher's attention must be given to students with non-collegiate backgrounds, with marginal command of basic skills, and with weak records in their previous academic training. Working with such students makes great demands on all the skills a superior teacher must possess. It makes a further demand in seeing teaching in the larger social context in which the college operates. **Career development in the community college needs to keep in mind these special demands and special opportunities.**

The support of junior college teachers able to communicate what they learn by close association with the real world is particularly important. There is no reason the junior college faculty and students should be cut off from the four-year college and university. Exchange programs between faculty members for short periods would be beneficial to both kinds of institutions. Graduate students in the university might do profitable apprentice teaching in the community colleges. And in the many areas where community colleges are reasonably close to major university centers, opportunities within these centers to add to the community college students' educational experiences should not be lost sight of. In many ways, the four-year colleges and universities have much to gain from granting the community colleges full recognition as an important part of higher education. There are mutual beneifts to be gained from assisting in developing and in drawing upon the teaching expertise and experience of the community college faculty.

Predominantly Negro Colleges

Teaching in the predominantly Negro colleges has some of the characteristics to be found in the community colleges. Shelbert Smith, director of an AAUP project for developing institutions supported by the Ford Foundation, provides a concise description of these schools:

> Presently, 34 of the 112 predominantly Negro institutions are public and enroll approximately one-half of all the Negro students. All but eight (8) are in the South. The approximately 160,000 students in the predominantly Negro schools represent 60% of all Negro students in higher education. Approximately 10,000 graduates are produced each year by the predominantly Negro institutions. Approximately 30% of the faculty in the predominantly Negro colleges and universities have the earned doctorate, as contrasted with 51% as a national average. Faculty salarics at the predominantly Negro institutions average $2,000-3,000 lower than the average in all institutions. However, the student cost at the predominantly Negro institutions is only about $100 a year less than the national average. Expectantly, in view of the social changes that are occurring, the predominantly Negro colleges and universities will have a difficult time recruiting and retaining quality students and faculty.

In May, 1970, the project co-sponsored a conference in Atlanta involving faculty members from a dozen Negro colleges in the South. The theme of the conference was "Improving the Learning-Teaching Experience." Though career development was not the focus of the discussion, the teacher and his or her impact upon the student was clearly the matter of greatest importance to the participants. Professor Leonard Archer spoke to the present quandary which faces not only these institutions but many others: "In the old days, in the church-related Black college, teachers and students worked together, lived together, ate together, prayed together, and played together. But who can bring them together again?" Similarly, the qualities that Professor Julius Taylor offered as being most important for a good teacher to possess are surely universal qualities: competence, concern or compassion, commitment, and enthusiasm.

As regards the specific development of teachers in and for the Negro institutions, a number of generalizations can be made.

Need for Funds

Foremost are all those matters which get neglected when an institution is chronically short of funds. The exhortations made to have institutions set aside fixed percentages of a total budget for faculty development may sound hollow in institutions where financial needs are so great. Financial support is clearly crucial to the development and maintenance of effective teachers in the Negro colleges as it is to other aspects of their functioning. Nor is it necessary to single out just the Negro colleges. The financial plight of small liberal arts colleges and the lack of internal flexibility that goes with small size is a grave problem all higher education faces. State and national support of Negro colleges is insufficient, private support of the magnitude needed is not forthcoming, and assistance programs of various kinds touch only the surface.

Having said that, it may seem foolish to go further. But the participants at the Atlanta conference, teachers whose careers have been devoted to institutions in varying degrees of financial crises, did go beyond their financial needs. More than many groups of faculty members, they were able to move from immediate problems and vexations to consider how teaching might be enhanced even under existing conditions.

More Opportunities

More opportunities for faculty members to proceed on with scholarly work or to gain experience beyond the confines of their campus are a necessity in the Negro college. Lacking the prestige of larger institutions, the research connections with major graduate schools, these institutions do not afford faculty even an equal opportunity to compete in the national market for leaves, grants, and research support. Exchange programs, on the face of it useful for faculty members at both institutions, have some drawbacks which compromise their utility. Faculty members from outside cannot serve the Negro college very well if they come to it as a way of satisfying either curiosity or guilt. Nor is the scholarly competence of an exchange professor likely to say much about his effectiveness on the Negro college campus. Conversely, the Negro college faculty member's needs may not be met by exchange with another institution. A different teaching assignment somewhere else may not be a source of growth for a teacher who has already been teaching too much and having too little time for thought or reflective study.

Negro college faculty members also mention the need for instilling confidence in many of their colleagues. Shelbert Smith has observed that "the teacher in the predominantly Negro institution is reluctant to change patterns of teaching for reasons of insecurity and feelings of frustration in his own work." Such teachers cannot merely be exposed to opportunities even if such opportunities were forthcoming. A prior step of using the assured talent that exists in the Negro colleges to lift the morale of the rest of the faculty is probably a first necessity. Development of faculty members in Negro colleges greatly depends on support from the outside and in ways that will make it attractive to the faculty member whose insecurity may reject the possibility of development.

Particular Strengths and Conflicts

Another very evident strain in the Atlanta discussions was the strong feeling among the participants that their particular teaching skills and experiences were not being used. They felt, for example, that the recently-awakened interest in disadvantaged students usually manifested itself in grants to major schools, in disregard of the fact that such institutions were least knowledgeable about the problems. The faculty members I have talked with do have attitudes and skills which need to be given wider visibility. "Take the student where he is and move with him from there," is a good maxim for any teacher, but it is a kind of basic stance for teachers who deal with students having difficulties in learning. Teachers in the Negro colleges are often more sensitive to the devices by which students evade learning, more aware of the fears of students, and of their need for figures they can identify with. And though these faculty members had marked disagreements about the uniqueness of the Negro experience or of the wisdom of dwelling upon that experience, they had no disagreement that Negro students and faculty had more to contribute to higher education than the existing opportunities made possible.

Though the urban Negro college is very much drawn into the community, Negro colleges in the south have in the past been separated from the community. The Negro faculty member is very vulnerable, right now, to conflicting demands of campus and community and to the conflicts which characterize all approaches, in white schools or black, to minority education. "My point is," one faculty woman argued, "black is no longer enough for Blacks to concentrate on." Nevertheless, the careers of those Negro faculty members, and those from other minorities as well, who rise to some prominence are threatened by too many demands upon them. For these demands pile upon the already heavy burden of choices that the Negro faculty member must make as to the very direction higher education for his students should take. The southern Negro college also feels the effects of having faculty members and able students attracted away from the region by competing offers from outside.

Finally, Negro colleges in the South are strongly in need of the kind of development which would make governing structures less autocratic and paternal. Conscious career development is not likely to flourish where the bulk of academic decisions are made by the administration. The development of teachers goes best in an atmosphere in which they are given responsibility. The faculty member in the Negro college needs an enhancement of freedom from both outside pressures and internal ones. As members of the conference said, the needed changes are social ones as well as institutional.

Some of what has been said can be applied to other minorities — students and faculty — who are seeking more access to higher education. Though there are a few institutions predominantly for Indian students and some with predominant enrollments of Mexican-Americans, neither of these groups is adequately represented among the faculty. Dealing with the education of minority students is still plagued by not knowing what to do, or not being in agreement about it, or being unwilling or unable to do those things upon which there is agreement. Faculty members at all institutions have been drawn into these problems. The end of discrimination, wider opportunities, more sensitivity to individual needs, the creation of alternate learning structures, the enlargement of post-educational job opportunities — these are probably aims all can agree upon. The Opportunity Fellowships established by the Danforth Foundation grew out of the conclusion that "the shortage of professional talent among Blacks, Puerto Ricans, Mexican-Americans, Indian-Americans, and poor whites was related to the dearth of persons of such backgrounds in American graduate schools, which in turn was related to the low income, lack of educational incentive, and racial or ethnic disabilities which characterized them." The fellowship programs established in 1967 at Vanderbilt, University of Cincinnati, UCLA, and the University of Wisconsin provide guidance and experience for further extension of opportunities. It is not irrelevant to the improvement of teaching that all four of these institutions identified committed students and concerned faculty as the main factors in the success of their programs.

Women on the Faculty

No one can visit college campuses today and not see reflections of the woman question. The common observation that women are more engaged specifically in teaching in the colleges and universities than men was borne out by my own campus visits. Though I made no exact count, women seemed to be a substantial part of the audiences who came out to discuss various aspects of improving teaching. Any consideration of improving teaching has good reason for examining the possibilities of enhancing the careers of women in the academic profession.

Two main sources of data about the place of women in the profession are Jessie Bernard's *Academic Women* (1964) and Helen Astin's *The Woman Doctorate in America* (1969). According to these studies, women do spend a greater proportion of their time teaching. Helen Astin's study gives comparative figures of 50 percent for women Ph.D.'s to 33 percent for men, and 25 percent of time devoted to research for women as against 41 percent for men. Jessie Bernard argues convincingly that women also gain more satisfactions from teaching and tend to value teaching higher than men. Both books offer evidence that women represent a kind of teaching potential which is not being fully used. Jessie Bernard's 1964 study is cautious about supporting this last statement, for she rightly argues that one has to set certain standards for how many women should be in the academic profession before one can claim they are under- or over-represented. The percentage of women faculty members has fluctuated from 20 to 30 percent for 70 years, and is probably around 20 percent, lower than in the 1950's, right now. A steady rise in the percentage accompanied the woman suffrage movement, but since 1930, the percentages have returned to the 18 to 22 percent level. These facts support other evidence that the years of expansion in higher education since World War II have been strongly dominated by men. In reporting on her current study of women faculty members in Minnesota colleges and universities, Ruth Eckert writes, "Comparisons with findings from the earlier study suggest that women are actually *more* disadvantaged now than they were in the mid-1950's, whether this is judged by percentage on college staffs, academic ranks, or scholarly preparation and productivity."

Cutbacks and Facts

The over-supply of Ph.D.'s and the tight market for jobs has already had its impact on women teachers. For cutbacks in academic personnel always begin at the fringes, and this is where a large number of women have been employed. The expansive period of the sixties enlarged the opportunity for the part-time woman teacher. But with choices now having to be made as to using academic women as part-time teachers or graduate assistants working toward higher degrees, most departments will incline toward the latter. In addition, it will take strong pressures from the women themselves to offset the inclination to favor male applicants for admission to Ph.D. programs whose enrollments have been cut back.

It is hard not to be shocked by the facts of women's employment by colleges and universities. They earn less, occupy the lower ranks, serve chiefly in the less prestigious institutions, teach the lowest level of courses, and rarely move into administrative positions. Though over half of graduate students in such a broad field as English are women, only about a fourth of the doctorates are, and the percentage of women full professors on the faculty of major universities shrinks to 4 to 5 percent. In the physical sciences all of these figures drop sharply with the percentage of women on physical science faculties in major universities dropping to 1 to 2 percent. Aside from the particulars of her employment, the modal picture of the academic woman, as stated by Jessie Bernard, is of "a very bright person so far as test-intelligence is concerned, but compliant rather than aggressive, from an above average social class background, and with a major interest in the humanities."

The relationship between women teachers and the improvement of teaching is frustratingly circular: an improvement in undergraduate teaching is likely to affect the position of women in the university favorably and the bettering of women's position in the university is likely to lead to improvements in undergraduate teaching. But even as regards improving teaching, a number of qualifications need to be made. Neither teaching nor the careers of women may be greatly advanced by the continued pattern of large

numbers of women accepting and enjoying "fringe benefit status."
Jessie Bernard describes this group:

> For the most part, they are the wives of deans,
> professors, instructors, graduate students, or often, even of
> townsmen. They constitute an elastic labor pool, hired and
> furloughed as needed. They carry a large share of the
> backbreaking load of introductory work in English com-
> position, modern languages, history, mathematics, natural
> sciences and the like.

From one point of view, a view supported by many professio-
nally-oriented women professors, the acceptance of such status helps
account for the generally unfavorable treatment of women. They are
not "professional," either by comparison with the great majority of
male colleagues or with the substantial number of women fully
committed to the profession. They let themselves be seen chiefly as
"teachers" and in their love of doing it and the limited opportunities
for being able to, accept low wages, bottom-level classes, lack of
tenure or rank, and the like. In these respects, they confirm the
secondary position assigned to teaching in the lower division. They
comprise a large number of the women on a given faculty, but since
they do not have a full place in the total professional work of the
department nor in the important educational deliberations of the
university, they add to the general tendency of a male-dominated
faculty and administration to regard all women faculty members as
not fully "professional."

The two kinds of academic women — the fringe benefit ones
just described and those fully professional — raise important
problems, both for the woman teacher and for higher education. The
advantages of having a highly-intelligent, adequately-trained, reasonably happy part-time faculty are great. In a period of expanding
enrollments, such a force is indispensable. At the same time, its
presence can lead to many abuses. From the woman's point of view,
availability often encourages exploitation, and the general disadvan-
tageous position of women to men as regards salaries, rank,
advancement, class assignments, may be a consequence of such
availability-exploitation. On the other hand, the institution which
refuses to exploit faces accusations of discrimination against women
when it may principally be a choice between full-time or part-time
appointments.

When one thinks of the numbers of highly-qualified women in
an academic community whose position as women keeps them from

full time academic commitments, it seems prejudicial to them and a waste of resources not to find ways to use them. When one sees how the lower division — not only in teaching, but in curriculum, financial support, philosophy, innovation — has been cut off from the rest of the university program, one is not so sure that the use of graduate students and women in the fringe benefit status has not been a major cause. The great advantage of the full-time professional over the part-time faculty member, woman or man, is that the university's on-going health is not only dependent upon the research and teaching that goes on there, but upon the intelligence, time and energy the faculty gives to the institution as a whole. If the project asks that more faculty members (predominantly male) commit themselves to undergraduate teaching, it seems neither consistent nor wise to argue for heavy support of university teaching with part-time personnel. And as the project has argued against exploitation of graduate students, it must also argue against the exploitation of women, even, when in both cases, the end of exploitation may mean a curtailment in available positions.

What I am emphasizing here is not the general choice of women for teaching as against research or administration, nor the qualities that women bring to teaching. Rather, it is the loss to an institution which results when too many of the faculty have major commitments elsewhere. The teaching that goes on in the university should be a unitary activity: what happens in the classroom needs to have maximum impact — more than it does now — on institutional policies, growth, development. The interaction of faculty and student, faculty and colleagues, are important to the quality of academic life. Part-time employment, whether occasioned by being both housewife and teacher or by being both off-campus consultant and teacher, reduces the chance of this kind of unitary development which I think is vital for the improvement of college teaching.

This does not mean that the academic woman has no choice but a full-time commitment to a college or university position. It does emphasize the need for flexibility in institutional policies and practices which have been emphasized elsewhere. The end of nepotism rules, stated or unstated, might bring an end to the practice of evading such rules by putting the wife in a part-time, subsidiary position. A more flexible leave policy might meet some of the needs of child-bearing and rearing than sabbatical programs now commonly provide. An increased receptivity to individuals entering the profession by other routes than graduate school training following close upon undergraduate education would enlarge opportunities for married women. And the thrust toward greater flexibility in kinds of study, off-campus experience and teaching, different teaching structures, different patterns of course and credits and grades all seem in the direction of permitting more women to be fully committed professionally and to still be wives and mothers as men now are husbands and fathers.

We would not be part-time, fringe-benefit teachers of lowly courses, I can hear women say, if sex discrimination — in the home and in the universities — had not forced it upon us. Institutions, departments, professional associations — all have been responsible for sex discrimination in the appointment and employment of women. Such discrimination seems to be more pronounced as one ascends the scale of institutional prestige. Ironically too, the research emphasis of such institutions has given women the principal effective weapon against discriminatory practices. Against the threat of losing large government grants, even such institutions as Harvard have been able to look at women faculty members in a more favorable light. It may be that the generalizations that have been made about women as faculty members — their compliance, satisfaction in working with people, their preferences in subject matter areas, even their interest in teaching — might experience considerable change if women were ever to operate, even within academic contexts, free of discrimination.

The realities that women face in choosing college teaching as a career can be seen from another perspective in the efforts of the Woodrow Wilson Fellowship Foundation to interest young men and women in college teaching careers. An analysis of the data disclosing career patterns of Woodrow Wilson fellows clearly shows that women, regardless of field, size of fellowship support, or quality of their undergraduate college, are simply much greater risks than men. A 1966 report on the careers of the 1958-60 fellows gives a "success ratio," defined in terms of the percentage of elected fellows who enter college teaching, of about 70 percent. The "success ratio" for female graduate students was about 43 percent. Of 780 fellows whose positions in 1966 were known and who were not employed as teachers or were still in the graduate school, 211 were housewives. "Short of excluding all girls from the fellowship competition," the research report stated, "there is little which can be done to prevent the housewife type of loss." Some of these women will resume teaching careers later on, but the immediate loss illustrates one of the specific problems in considering career development of faculty women. The Danforth's graduate fellowship program for women is a recognition of the precise need to assist women who have interrupted graduate work or teaching to resume their academic careers. A higher education in which teaching were regarded as worthy of the full commitment of male and female intelligence, imagination, and sympathies, could gain much from full involvement of women, not just as "devoted teachers" but as professionals devoted to the art of teaching.

As regards the individual institution, a satisfactory faculty development program must not only deal with the well-being of the generality of faculty, but with such specific and yet unrealized potentialities as are represented in the teaching force outside the dominant male, white, conventionally-trained, research-oriented, and competitive professor. There is no question that though an end to discrimination would help both women and members of minority groups to develop as teachers, that alone is not enough. Patterns of development must be looked at before they enter graduate school. Special incentives and kinds of support will need to be provided to increase the numbers going on with advanced training and the numbers who are able to go on to an advanced degree. An attention to teaching in the graduate school would be particularly useful to both groups. Some movement away from the single scholarly program, the certification by Ph.D. degree, the disinclination in hiring to see beyond the doctoral universities and the professional disciplines would also help. If, within the university, discrimination in hiring practices would cease and a more varied and interesting faculty would come into existence, there would still be a need to draw faculty members into a common interest in teaching and to end the separate kingdoms by which we have, in the past, been able to find a place for women and other minority professors. The strength these individuals is in the high priority many of them already give to teaching, the stored-up energies, if you will, that can go into active participation in improving college teaching.

8. Leadership

Developing and maintaining effective teachers, encouraging effective teaching, and working toward a faculty development program which would do both should gain wide support on most campuses. The various suggestions this booklet has made for moving in these directions are not likely to be strongly opposed. The difficulty is in putting useful measures into effect. Even knowing where we want to go, how do we get there from here?

The first response is to look for sources of power on campus. Unfortunately and despite all the jockeying for power going on, no one seems to have any. Power is dissipated throughout the bureaucracy. In the multiversity, according to Clark Kerr, even the president is mostly a mediator. Nevertheless, colleges and universities continue to run, and individuals in administrative positions still use the powers they may feel uneasy about asserting. The responsibilities of deans, department chairmen, and higher administrative officials have been mentioned in previous chapters. Here, the intention is to directly address individuals who do have power on campus and to charge them with the necessity of providing leadership.

Sources of Power — The President

Let us begin with power at the top — the president.

Clark Kerr, one of the few modern presidents with a public identity, claimed that "Hutchins was the last of the giants in the sense that he was the last of the university presidents who really tried to change his institution and higher education in any fundamental way." Mediation, initiation, the opportunity to persuade, are, in Kerr's opinion, the only ways presidents have of exercising an influence upon the multiversity.

Harold Dodds is neither so certain that the days of the giants are past nor that modern presidents cannot be leaders. "If, as a

115

genre," he writes in *The Academic President — Educator or Caretaker?*, "presidents of the present are deficient, it is in their capacity to escape being overwhelmed by managerial operations, to excite, to inspire, and to lift leadership to the plane of statesmanship."

There is no need here to join in the general debate. Certainly the size of the universities, the multiplication of all kinds of voices asking for public attention, the absorption of the university into American managerial enterprises, make it difficult for any college president to be heard. Occasionally, such as during specific crises, a president of a sufficiently prominent university or college will make public statements which gain wide attention. In peaceful times, such voices seldom reach the public, and lacking public attention gain little attention on campus. Kerr's acceptance of a managerial role for the president gives one explanation for the silence. Corporation heads seldom make memorable utterances, their prose, like that of university presidents, being formed or polished by others and confined to house organs and reports to stockholders.

To my mind, that is a sorry position for presidents to have reached. The "position" of president, regardless of the man filling that position, has power, and not to use that power openly in the interest of higher education is a major dereliction of duty.

Formulating educational policy, shaping his own ideas about education, are more important than the rhetorical exercises in official publications would make them seem. Formulation depends upon having such ideas, and that is a responsibility which cannot be delegated. It is either a president's choice or passive acceptance of current executive style that someone else (or a team) should provide the imagination. Another wing will lay on the rhetoric. A third phalanx surveys the market and sets up the channels. As necessary as this may seem, the necessity is of the same order as that which causes most professors to lecture and to give to teaching about what tradition and personal ease incline them to.

A president should have one or two or three specific *educational* plans he would like to see carried out. He should give them sufficient details to make them visible, expose them openly to members of the academic community, and, if they seem to hold up under scrutiny, push hard to get them into effect. There is not an institution in the country whose teaching would not benefit from the direct and purposeful interest of the president. And yet, during my travels to big institutions and small, I met few presidents who seemed to have educational ideas and sufficient interest to put them across. Leo Nussbaum, president of Coe, was called to my attention by many faculty members as chiefly responsible for invigorating the climate for teaching and learning there. Robert Davis at Idaho State is probably more visible in connection with educational activities in that institution than he is with state legislators and sources of grants. David Mathews, I have been told, president of the University of Alabama, is largely responsible for the establishment of New College on that campus. None of these are what could be called national spokesmen for higher education, but educational leadership is as necessary within individual institutions as emanating from the great university centers.

Academic Vice-Presidents

Vice-presidents are created to make it possible for the president to concentrate his limited person and energies on the major tasks. Teaching, it seems to me is always a major task, and the responsibility for it can little afford to be delegated by the president. Nevertheless, the office of academic vice-president has tended to take over this function. If it operates well, it can be the major source of power in support of teaching.

The academic vice-president should be the faculty's man. And since responsibility for teaching ultimately rests with the faculty, it is necessary to have the faculty's man working actively for it. The academic vice-presidency also requires a man of some educational breadth and one who can respond to the varied interests of the faculty. Programs coming from the academic vice-president's office may be assumed to represent the faculty's interest and thus gain faculty support and confidence.

Specific responsibility for a campus-wide faculty development program probably rests, then, with the academic vice-president. It could as easily be a "president's program," though even then, the details of its functioning would likely come into the vice-president's hands. A proposal to institute a career development program could hardly be improved upon as a way of bringing administration and faculty together for the common good. Since it so obviously is in the faculty interest, it is possible to have a great deal of the impetus and the actual design come from the top. And it provides an opportunity to put the administration in the role administration is supposed to play: that of saving the faculty for their primary duties of teaching and scholarship.

Establishing a Career Development Program

The emphasis on administrative leadership is not meant to imply that even the most beneficial of measures should be forced upon, even thrust upon a faculty. Establishing a career development program cannot be done heavy-handedly, but it cannot be done at all without strong administrative action. I suspect an individual could not be given an independent income for life without feeling he should have been involved, somehow, in working it out. Faculties are very jealous about being involved in all matters that affect their daily functioning. But administrators can be so uneasy about faculty participation that they fail to do enough to relieve the faculty from unnecessary administrative involvement.

There is no reason, for example, to involve the faculty endlessly in hammering out the details of a career development program. An administrative team in which faculty might be employed as consultants could better work out the particulars. Where the faculty might be most involved is in giving their strongest support to the program when the administrative sponsors fight for budgetary support.

Money is the central problem that the academic vice-president's office must face. The faculty cannot face it; faculties have very little to say about the division of budget at the apportionment level. Someone in high places must argue for a principle that has yet to be established in higher education despite the fact that it is a commonplace of business practice: **a portion of the budget must be allotted specifically to development, and faculty development must claim a large part of that allotment.**

Unfortunately, even under such a plan, teaching itself may lay little claim to the available funds. Universities oriented toward research and operating under strong college and departmental autonomy are likely to see faculty development in other ways than strengthening teaching. What I am arguing for is money specifically apportioned to the development of faculty members as teachers and deliberately kept away from research proposals and designs.

What would even ½ of 1 percent, $250,000 from a $50,000,000 budget, provide? A fourth of that amount could staff a modest center for teaching, provide the salary that could attract a highly respected and competent member of the faculty to direct the operation for a year and assure him of enough clerical support to handle the important informational function of such an office. Given the right man, an amount equal to the cash outlay would probably be forthcoming from the initiation of activities within colleges and departments basically using their own funds.

Another fourth could provide three university professorships, "teaching" professorships not responsible for the year to departments, not tied to other obligations for the period. Again, with the cooperation of departments, that number could easily be doubled.

Another fourth could go into a grants program in support of course development, innovations in teaching, professional development of teachers. Sixty grants of one thousand dollars each could result in a consequential infusion of better courses, better methods into a university curriculum.

Another fourth could be reserved as a departmental incentive budget. Departments which, for example, proposed an effective program for training their graduate assistants might be given substantial help. The amount, here, would not go far, but it would still be sufficient to assist small departments in upgrading teaching in specific ways and to support some activities in large departments which had not been undertaken for lack of interest and/or lack of funds.

One could imagine cutting up the pie in various ways. The trick is to get at the pie. It is not convincing to say that the general fund cannot be stretched that far. In the big universities, it already stretches to cover a good many matters less essential to the instructional program. What is necessary is administrative courage to argue for the amount at the highest level of apportionment and to keep it from disappearing in the budgeting process. Institutions are like individuals. What has to be purchased immediately has priority over what might be better in the long run. Big, showy, tangible possessions have priority over smaller expenditures which might improve the quality of life. The institution's budget, like an individual's, needs strong leadership, to defend it from itself.

It is not quite an impossible idea to propose to a faculty that individuals let the institution set aside a fixed sum — say $500 — for their own development. Not the new roof on the house, or the children's orthodontures, or the wife's pleadings, or the individual's desire just to have the sum in hand could gain access to it. It could, however, be freely drawn upon for those purposes the faculty member regarded as important for his development as a teacher. Thus he might look in on teaching at another place, might take a trip without having to trick up an invitation to a conference, might make a set of slides, might entertain his students. The individual, of course, would have to convince himself that while it was money coming from his own salary, it was money that would otherwise not be available for these purposes. It would offer a kind of sanctioned self-indulgence in matters helpful to the development of one's professional self. If the institution were willing to go a step further, and propose to match the amount for all those willing to set up such a fund, the chance of faculty acceptance might rise and at a cost probably within the ½ of 1 percent of the budget proposed for career development.

Using Assisting Personnel

The size of institutions has multiplied the number of administrative personnel at all levels. Assistants to the various vice-presidents, associate deans, assistant department chairmen, are commonplace and necessary. But it might be a wiser use of the necessary increase in positions to give some of those in subordinate position very specific assignments. It was no accident that the teaching assistantship program at the University of Utah gained some badly needed support when an associate academic vice-president, Charles Monson, was able and willing to give specific attention to that program. Prior to that time, the grievances were being felt at the departmental level, some pressures at the dean's level, and very little at the higher administrative level where overall university needs were viewed in relation to budget. Given that specific problem to deal with, the associate vice-president could gain first-hand acquaintance with the teaching assistant program, get the facts about salaries, the student credit hours taught, the competing priorities, and make an effective case at a high administrative level for broad institutional support. Institutions entering upon career development programs, even those backed by the president or academic vice-president, would be wise to invest the time of a specific administrative officer in getting the program established and being responsible for its functioning.

The Dean's Function

The dean's function in improving the possibilities for faculty development is different from that of the president or vice-president. He cannot speak to the whole university, and his interests are in building or maintaining a college, not in developing a faculty or in encouraging teaching. The position of dean of a large college of arts and sciences has some of the dimensions of the presidency of a liberal arts college, but that college still operates within a framework which limits his vision, his control of budget, and his scope of action.

Colleges within a university, and the deans of such colleges, are dominated by a professionalism which often works as much against undergraduate teaching as for it. Deans of a certain kind are even more zealous than department chairmen to get the big names as a means of shoring up weak departments or of enhancing the reputations of strong ones. How little the luminary is to teach is probably a major factor in the negotiations. At best, the dean must seem to be treating departments equitably, must look to all the aspects of maintaining a strong and smoothly functioning operation. Removed from both student and faculty except for contact in the context of administrative duties, he is most likely among those in administrative positions to become the functionary. Functionaries do not often function as leaders. A dean has neither the power to institute nor access to the financial support for a broad faculty development program. And though he could establish such within his own college, or even collaborate with other deans to work out broader programs, such programs, I think, would be strongly subject to departmental pressures and to the pressures that would give the enhancing of outside professional reputation higher priority than the improvement of teaching.

I am looking at a detailed manual for department chairmen in a large college in a major university. The dean's responsibilities are set forth with care. The dean determines major policies and the implementation of programs, oversees the instructional program "among departments whose areas of responsibility coincide, relate or overlap," assists chairmen in the development of individual faculty members, and consults chairmen in matters of collective development of various groups of faculty. He also has an associate dean for instruction, an associate dean for research and academic personnel, and an executive office for budget and planning. The duties of the first concern programs, courses, new offerings, faculty fellowships and innovative projects. The duties of the second are chiefly with organized research units, individual grants and contracts, and with appointments of temporary and visiting academic personnel. The duties of the third concern budgets, studies of space use and needs, records and studies of enrollments, staff and workload, and special assignment of teaching assistants to meet unexpected demands.

It is a neat enough structure, but in language, certainly, and in actuality, I would guess, it hardly touches upon the realities of teaching. With its lumping of "research" with "academic personnel" it does not seem even to be very close to academic personnel as teachers. To be sure, there is a separate structure under an Associate Dean for Student Services which seems to have a lot to do with students, but the roster of duties for the eight assistant deans are devoted to suspension of college rules, difficult academic problems, probation and dismissal, readmission, and special major programs.

I think it is fair to say that this organizational structure, typical of large, major universities, reveals a fragmentation of responsibilities, an assignment to department chairmen of almost all responsibilities for teaching and teachers, and a maximum of the kind of administrative involvement which gets in the way of the dean's exercising educational leadership.

Nevertheless, the dean or the dean's office is in a position to assist greatly in the development of faculty members as teachers. We have already mentioned the dean as a likely person to whom faculty members turn for professional counsel. The dean's office does gain acquaintance with many faculty members out of department contexts and learns a good deal about what motivates and hinders performance. Thus, the dean is in a very good position to serve an active, initiating role as well as a reviewing and overseeing one with respect to department chairmen and development of departmental faculty. Through the processing of appointments and review of advancement recommendations, the dean's office has about as complete a record of faculty personnel as the department chairman, and has additional information about faculty personnel within the college. A program for faculty development emanating from the dean's office could be more personal, work more closely with departments, and aim at specific objectives that might make it superior to a university-wide program.

I can envision the dean's office doing some of the following things:

1. **Shape and staff the program of development for beginning faculty members in the college. This might include:**

- *reducing loads across the college for first-year teachers.*

- *working with various departments to put first or second-year teachers into team-teaching relationships with other departments.*

- *sponsoring informal discussions of teaching among new and experienced faculty members across the college.*

- *providing incentives in money or released-time grants for young faculty members (not just beginning teachers) to develop courses and their skill as teachers.*

2. **Establish an informal but active counseling center for faculty. The functions of such a center might include:**

- *periodic discussions with faculty member of his or her aspirations, needs, frustrations, and fears as a teacher. These should be matters of course rather than of crisis.*

- *engagement of faculty members at all ranks in ways in which their specific teaching enthusiasms might be served.*

- *specific, personal attention to faculty members reaching their last years of service.*

3. Take responsibility for gathering and disseminating information about teaching. This might include:

- *distributing useful outside articles, reports, studies, and bibliographies concerned with teaching to department chairmen and faculty.*

- *gathering and disseminating information about teaching practices within the college.*

- *sponsoring specific studies of various aspects of teaching practices within the college, e.g. use and effectiveness of lectures; methods of examination; measures of student achievement, and the like.*

4. Establish and maintain various programs to give visibility to teaching and to enhance the possibilities for the career teacher. This might include:

- *sponsoring interchange among department chairmen about teaching and about the development of faculty members as teachers.*

- *sponsoring visits of distinguished teachers from nearby institutions to talk with faculty and students.*

- *encouraging student and alumni interest in teaching and supporting student efforts to improve teaching.*

- *taking responsibility for a systematic program of evaluating teaching, using student ratings, class visitation, and other means.*

5. Set up a review and reward system for departments based on the department's effectiveness in developing and maintaining excellence in teaching.

This should be sufficient to indicate kinds of activities which might come from the dean's office. Above all, the dean of a college needs to get out of a passive role. As members of the San Francisco conference agreed, the dean's responsibility to teaching is to find out what useful things are going on and to encourage and reward them, and to encourage some things which should be going on but aren't.

The Department Chairman

The department chairman, like the dean, can work closely with faculty and students to support teachers and teaching. In carrying out his responsibilities for faculty appointment, retention, promotion, and salary increases, he cannot help but have a strong influence on teaching. His efforts should not, however, be confined even to matters as important as these. His attention to the department's curriculum, to teaching assignments and teaching loads, to ascertaining the strengths and weaknesses of individual teachers, to providing the necessaries in equipment, clerical help, and information, to offering encouragement and motivation — all these and others have a direct impact on faculty performance. In addition, there are many ways in which the department chairman's carrying out of his responsibilities affects student performance. And finally, there is the leadership by example — the place he gives teaching in his own professional life — which has a strong impact within the department, on students and faculty alike.

It may be that since so many of the chairman's every day responsibilities deal with teaching and faculty development, no additional ways should be suggested to add to an already heavy burden. But busyness is everyone's burden, and unless conscious attention is given to specific matters, many useful tasks remain undone. With the common practice of rotating chairmanships, there is a chance that a new man's energies, for a time at least, will extend to a wider range than housekeeping matters. Like other administrative officers, the chairman should have some specific ways in which he would like to affect teaching for the better. If he does have, he will probably find the time to carry them out.

He might, for example:

- Use his acquaintance with preparing teachers for the public schools in a variety of ways to affect teaching in the department.

- Set up definite programs of exchange of teaching assignments, guest lecturing, and class visitations.

- Constantly try to increase the possibilities of faculty member's being informed about what is going on.

- Arrange ways outside of class and course contexts for the faculty to gain insight as to their impact upon students.

- Work directly with beginning teachers and graduate assistants to develop their competence as teachers.

- Furnish feedback to teachers and students about how teaching fares in the reward system.

- Provide opportunities for discussions of teaching, exposure to different teaching styles, innovation in teaching.

- Solicit ideas for new courses and teaching practices.

- Provide departmental recognition for different kinds of teaching excellence.

- Use his own limited teaching time to explore new ways of structuring classes and stimulating learning.

One other responsibility falls very heavily upon the department chairman: that of subverting the department itself. No one is in a better position to break down the barriers that separate disciplines, though it will take much more than a chairman to move American universities toward interdisciplinary work. Nevertheless, chairmen are in that advantageous position for exercising leadership, namely, that a man may be listened to if he appears to be arguing against his own self-interest. I cannot say that my visits of the past two years have made me join those, like Paul Dressel, who locate many of the ills of the university in the departmental structure. Yet, I respect that position, for one cannot work very long in the university without becoming aware of the baneful influence of the department.

Departments have a very strong responsibility for the narrowness and professionalism of undergraduate programs and for the unchallenged position of specialized research in the graduate school. I have already mentioned the necessity for broadening the base for judgment of faculty performance beyond that which the department and department faculty provide. And implicit in what has been said about the usefulness of teaching in other departments and of inter-departmental programs is the necessity of breaking down department barriers to such efforts. Nevertheless, departments, if they have not themselves become too large, are one of the few remaining effectively operating sub-units within the large university. Structurally, departments suffer from being both too large and too small, but any re-examination of the departmental structure should have firm ways of arriving at functioning groupings of students and teachers before giving up on the departments.

As regards the improvement of teaching, the department is the closest one can come in influencing teaching practices short of working with individual faculty members. Department chairmen are in a position to work directly and effectively with the faculty. They are in a position to perceive some relationship between student development and the faculty's activities. And they are necessarily drawn into university-wide discussions of practices and policies much more than departmental faculty members. As I have accused presidents of failing to exercise their powers in the cause of education, I may accuse chairmen of exercising their powers to preserve departmental self-interest. If, as Clark Kerr has recently suggested, the emerging image of the president is that of academic statesmen, perhaps department chairmen can emerge as statesmen, too.

Students and Faculty

Faculty and student bodies can be helpful to the development of faculty members as teachers. Students and colleagues play an important part in a faculty member's job satisfactions and motivations. In a survey of 10,300 professors who had taken new positions in colleges across the country, "competency of colleagues" weighed more heavily in their choices than did salary, and congeniality of colleagues was said to be even more important than academic rank. Ruth Eckert's studies of job satisfactions found that the opportunity to work with college age youth, a liking for teaching, and promotion of students' development constitute a major source of satisfactions for college teachers. It is important, therefore, that any program of faculty development be accepted by the faculty and that the presence of such a program be made known to the students. Involving both in the program's development is probably the best way toward achieving both ends.

Faculty or university senates in a number of institutions have exercised leadership in examining aspects of teaching. Chronically impatient with the busy work of governance, members of university legislative bodies might be receptive to sponsoring studies, setting up task forces, even establishing continuing bodies in support of specific aspects of career development and the improvement of teaching. In the sensitive matter of evaluating teaching, senates are perhaps the best bodies to give direction and to gain acceptance for such efforts. Senates have their own problems of leadership which have not become simpler with the addition of students to such bodies. But the renewed interest in this branch of university governance, often with substantial addition of student representatives, increases the possibilities of leadership asserting itself within that structure.

With respect to improving teaching, students have been principally involved in course evaluations and in working with others in the academic community to arrive at awards for distinguished teachers. By means of membership on committees, and in university senates, and through creation of student advisory boards within departments and colleges, students have had increasing impact on academic practices. There are many ways in which students could be brought into the process of developing and maintaining effective teachers. Developing courses, for example, could well be a student/faculty activity. More sophisticated ways of determining how students learn depend heavily upon student cooperation. Permitting students to teach as part of the means of instruction has possibilities. And gaining insight into one's development as a teacher can be immeasurably assisted by students.

With respect to leadership, the quiet academic year just past may not be a very good sign. Certain parts of the student body seem disaffected with the very idea of leadership. Things just happen; the "now" will take care of us, brothers and sisters all. Leaders become much less conspicuous in quiet times, and the withdrawal of vigorous student leadership making angry demands likewise diminishes the need for administrative or faculty leadership in response. The student riots at Columbia, for example, had the effect of calling forth leadership from faculty members who had never exercised that kind of leadership before. In speculating about how faculty behave outside of times of crisis, we are unfortunately confronted with those academic values that put great emphasis upon a faculty member's being a "leader" in his field but little emphasis upon his being an educational leader within an actual and immediate academic community.

We need such leaders, among the student body as well as the faculty. It would be the gravest loss to higher education if the ferment aroused by student unrest of the last seven or eight years were to disappear into a time of everyone minding his own business. The bigness of the universities excuses almost everyone within the metropolis from trying to come forward very far and at the same time creates in the small colleges a feeling of being so removed and hard pressed as to inhibit leadership there.

One of the possible ways of creating conditions in which leadership might arise among faculty and students is to create alternate learning structures within a college or university, or, for that matter, outside the campus confines. Despite the presence of colleges and departments, most faculty members work on campuses with uniform admission and graduation requirements and a high degree of sameness in curriculum, grading, methods of instruction, and the like. For many years, the honors college or program has provided an alternative attractive for both faculty and students. The growth of institutes and other loosely-organized sub-structures is another means by which faculty members have found environments more congenial to their development. The various cluster colleges comprise a third movement toward alternative structures for teaching and learning. Jerry Gaff's book, *The Cluster College,* makes this argument for the impact of such a collegiate structure:

> The problem of giving adequate recognition to the teaching skills of the faculty can be resolved by creating colleges specially designed to provide an undergraduate education, attracting faculty members who are committed to this mission, creating a setting in which the effectiveness of teachers can be known by their colleagues, and giving provosts of the college a hand in deciding whether and how to reward professors.
>
> The policy of raising educational policy to the forefront of faculty concerns can be resolved by articulating alternatives to the conventional practices, encouraging faculty members to try out the new teaching methods, and devising ways of sharing authority for policy decisions.

There are enough reasons in the mere growth of the universities for breaking up collegial and university structures into more meaningful sub-units. There are good reasons, also, in the diversity of students and the pressures they put on the universities to provide teaching-learning communities with which they can identify. In addition, the diversity of faculty and the need to provide congenial teaching environments for them is a reason for being receptive to alternative structures for learning. But perhaps most of all, the deliberate fostering of new structures of learning would necessitate faculty and students taking an active part in shaping teaching and learning and thereby increase the opportunities and possibilities for educational leadership of this kind.

A Career Development System

Supposing that administrative leadership were forthcoming, faculty and student cooperation assured, what kind of system for development of the faculty as teachers might emerge? Let me end this discussion by putting down some of the constituent elements:

1. **Financial support.** A specific apportionment of a percentage of a university's general operating fund to faculty development, and specific allotment within that apportionment for development of teachers and teaching.

2. **Presence of a definite system.** A system does not need to embrace all activities directed toward faculty development nor does it in itself assure effective results. But the creation of some regular, continuing program with identifiable characteristics seems essential.

3. **Lodging of responsibility with a high administrative officer.** A "president's program" might be ideal. The academic vice-presidency might do as well, with major responsibilities resting with a single administrative officer.

4. **The program itself should include:**

Attention to the needs of beginning teachers in the form of programs to develop teaching skills.

Grants and leaves designed to be available specifically to young teachers, those in mid-career, and older teachers. These might be on a competitive basis only within each category, and be specifically designed to best attract the attention and minister to the needs of faculty members in each group.

Departmental grants for programs which promise to improve instruction or add to the competence of faculty members as teachers.

Support of teachers not attached to departments and of non-collegiate structures for learning.

5. **Coordination with a system of teaching evaluation and assessment of student achievements.**

6. **Purposeful study and attention to the reward system within departments and the university to see that teaching rewards square with institutional policies.**

7. **Providing of information about and assistance in taking advantage of exchange programs for teachers, new teaching assignments, innovations on campus and elsewhere, and the workings of the faculty development system itself.**

Selective Bibliography

Adelson, J. The teacher as a model. *American Scholar,* Summer 1961, 383-406.

Allen, D. C. *The Ph.D. in English and American literature.* Holt, Rinehart and Winston, 1968.

Arden, E. A solution to the crisis in college teaching. *Liberal Education,* October 1965, 419-26.

Arnstein, G. E. *Design for an academic matching service.* American Association for Higher Education, 1967.

Arrowsmith, W. The future of teaching. In C. B. Lee ed., *Improving College Teaching,* American Council on Education, 1967, 57-71.

Astin, A. W. *The college environment.* American Council on Education, 1968.

Astin, A. W. How colleges are rated. *Change,* November-December 1970, 11, 85-86.

Astin, H. S. *The woman doctorate in America: origins, career, and family.* Russell Sage Foundation, 1969.

Axelrod, J., ed. *Graduate study for future college teachers.* American Council on Education, 1959.

Axelrod, J., et. al. *Search for relevance.* Jossey-Bass, 1969.

Barzun, J. *The American university: how it runs, where it is going.* Harper and Row, 1968.

Baskin, S., ed. *Higher education: some newer developments.* McGraw-Hill, 1965.

Bayer, A. E. *College and university faculty: A statistical description.* American Council on Education, 1970.

Berelson, B. *Graduate education in the United States,* McGraw-Hill, 1960.

Bernard, J. *Academic women.* Pennsylvania State University Press, 1964.

Birenbaum, W. M. *Overlive: power, poverty, and the university.* Delacorte Press, 1969.

Bolin, J. G., & McMurrain T. *Student-faculty ratios in higher education.* Institute of Higher Education, University of Georgia, 1969.

Brandis, R. The rehabilitation of university undergraduate teaching. *Educational Record,* Winter 1964, 56-63.

Brawer, F. *Personality characteristics of college and university faculty.* American Association of Junior Colleges, 1968.

Brick, M., & McGrath E. J. *Innovation in liberal arts colleges.* Teachers College Press, Columbia University, 1969.

Brickman, W. W., &Lehrer, S. *Conflict and change on the campus: the response to student hyperactivism.* School and Society Books, 1970.

Brown, D. Personality, college environments, and academic productivity. In N. Sanford ed., *The American college.* John Wiley and Sons, 1962, 536-562.

Brown, D. G. *The market for college teachers.* University of North Carolina Press, 1965.

Brown, D. G. *The mobile professors.* American Council on Education, 1967.

Caplow, T., & McGee, R. *The academic marketplace.* Basic Books, 1958.

Carmichael, O. C. *Graduate education: a critique and program.* Harper and Bros., 1961.

Chester, D. N., et. al. The organization of graduate studies and the training of graduates. *Universities Quarterly,* June 1964, 241-60.

Chickering, A. W. *Education and identity.* Jossey-Bass, 1969.

Clark, B. R. *The distinctive college: Antioch, Reed and Swarthmore.* Aldine, 1970.

Clark, B. R. Faculty organization and authority. In H. M. Vollmer and D. L. Mills, eds. *Professionalization.* Prentice-Hall, 1966, 282-291.

The college graduate: his early employment and job satisfaction. The College Placement Council, 1969.

Cooper, R. Improving college teaching and administration. In S. Baskin, ed. *Higher Education: some newer developments.* McGraw-Hill, 1965, 196-227.

Cooper, R., ed. *The two ends of the log.* University of Minnesota Press, 1958.

Crawford, S. C. A university-wide program of faculty development. *Educational Record,* Jan. 1961, 49-53.

Critique of a college. Swarthmore, 1967.

Demerath, N., Stephens, R., & Taylor, R. R. *Power, presidents and professors.* Basic Books, Inc., 1967.

Dennis, L., & Kauffman, F. *The college and the students.* American Council on Education, 1966.

Dennis, W. Creative productivity between the ages of 20 and 80 years. *Journal of Gerontology,* 21: 1-8, 1966.

DeVane, W. C. The responsibility of the modern professor. *Liberal Education,* March 1961, 5-13.

Dibden, A. *The academic deanship in American colleges and universities.* Southern Illinois University Press, 1968.

Dodds, H. W. *The academic president—educator or caretaker?* McGraw-Hill, 1962.

Dressel, P. L., Johnson, F. C., & Marcus, P. M. *The confidence crisis,* Jossey-Bass, 1970.

Dubin, R., & Taveggia, T. C. *The teaching-learning paradox.* University of Oregon, 1968.

Dunham, E. A. *Colleges of the forgotten Americans.* McGraw-Hill, 1969.

Dunham, R. E., Wright, P. S., & Chandler, M. O. *Teaching faculty in universities and four-year colleges.* U.S. Government Printing Office, 1966.

Dunlop, J. T., Chairman. Report of the committee on recruitment and retention of faculty. Faculty of Arts and Sciences, Harvard University, May 1, 1968.

Dykes, A. R. Faculty participation in academic decision making. American Council on Education, 1968.

Eble, K. E. *The recognition and evaluation of teaching.* Project to Improve College Teaching, 1970.

Eble, K. E. *Teaching, research, and professing,* Center for Study of Higher Education, University of Toledo, 1969.

Eckert, R. E., Stecklein, J. E., & Sagen, H. B. College faculty members view their jobs. *American Association of University Professors Bulletin,* December 1959, 513-528.

Eckert, R. E., Stecklein, J. E. *Job motivations and satisfactions of college teachers.* Cooperative Research Monograph No. 7. U.S. Government Printing Office, 1961.

Eckert, R. E., Williams, H. Y., Jr., & Anderson, D. H. *The University of Minnesota faculty: who serves and why?* University of Minnesota, 1970.

Eells, W. C. *College teachers and college teaching,* an annotated bibliography, 1957, Atlanta, Georgia: Southern Regional Education Board; First Supplement, 1959; Second Supplement, 1962; Third Supplement by M. L. Litton and W. H. Stickler, 1967.

Erikson, E. H. *Childhood and society.* Norton, 1950.

_____. Identity: youth and crisis. Norton, 1968.

Estrin, H. A. and Goode, D. *College and university teaching.* Wm. C. Brown, 1964.

Eurich, A. C., ed. *Campus 1980: the shape of the future in American higher education.* Delacorte Press, 1968.

Everett, W. *Graduate education today.* American Council on Education, 1965.

Felder, R. *Results of questionnaire on faculty work load.* ERIC ED 025 200, 1968.

Feldman, K. A., & Newcomb, T. M. *The impact of college on students.* Jossey-Bass, 1969.

Feuer, L. S. *The conflict of generations: the character and significance of student movements.* Basic Books, Inc., 1969.

Finger, F. W. "Professional problems": preparation for a career in college teaching. *American Psychologist,* November 1969, 1044-49.

Fischer, J. Is there a teacher on the faculty? *Harper's,* February 1965, 18, 20, 22, 24, 26, 28.

Fowler, J. M. Progress report of the commission on college physics for 1966-68. *American Journal of Physics,* November 1968, 1035-1067.

Furniss, W. Department and faculty profiles: an aid to judgment. *Liberal Education,* October 1963, 354-65.

Gaff, J. G. and associates. *The cluster college.* Jossey-Bass, 1970.

Gamson, Z. F. Performance and personalism in student-faculty relations. *Sociology of Education,* 1967, 279-301.

Gellerman, S. W. *Management by motivation.* American Management Association, 1968.

Gleazer, D. J., Jr. *This is the community college.* Houghton Mifflin Co., 1968.

Gordon, O. *Profess or perish.* Oregon State University Press, 1968.

Gouldner, A. W. Cosmopolitans and locals. *Administrative Science Quarterly,* December 1957, 281-306.

Graduate training for college teaching: a panel discussion, *AAUP Bulletin,* September 1960, 294-299.

Graham, P. A. Women in academe. *Science,* September 25, 1970, 1284-1290.

Gustad, J. W. *The career decisions of college teachers.* Southern Regional Education Board, 1970.

_____. Policies and practices in faculty evaluation. *Educational Record,* 42: 194-211, 1961.

Hammond, P. E., Meyer, J. W., & Miller, D. Teaching versus research: Sources of misperceptions. *Journal of Higher Education,* December 1969, 682-690.

Harcleroad, F. F., ed. *Issues of the seventies.* Jossey-Bass, 1970.

Hargens, L. L. Patterns of mobility of new Ph.D.'s among American academic institutions. *Sociology of Education,* 1969, 18-37.

Heiss, A. *Challenges to graduate schools.* Jossey-Bass, 1970.

Highet, G. *The art of teaching.* Knopf, 1950.

Hildebrand, M., & Wilson, R. C. Effective university teaching and its evaluation. Center for Research and Development in Higher Education, University of California, Berkeley, April 1970.

Hobbs, M. T. Teaching loads in selected liberal arts colleges. *Liberal Education,* December 1966, 418-421.

Hoyt, D. P., & Rawson, T. M. Why faculty leave KSU. Research Report No. 1, December 1968, Kansas State University, Office of Educational Research.

Ingraham, M. *The outer fringe.* University of Wisconsin Press, 1965.

Jacob, P. E. *Changing values in college.* Harper Brothers, 1957.

James, W. *Memories and studies.* Longman, Green, and Co., 1917, 329-347.

Jencks, C., & Riesman, D. *The academic revolution.* Doubleday, 1968.

Joughin, L. *Academic freedom and tenure.* University of Wisconsin Press, 1967.

Katz, J., & associates. *No time for youth.* Jossey-Bass, 1968.

Kelley, W., & Wilbur, L. *Teaching in the community-junior college.* Appleton-Century-Crofts, 1970.

Kerr, C. *The uses of the university.* Harvard University Press, 1963.

Kinnane, M. Attitudes of college students toward college teaching as a career. *Educational Record,* April 1962, 139-47.

Klapper, P. The professional preparation of the college teacher. *Journal of General Education,* April 1949, 228-44.

Knapp, R. Changing functions of the college professor. In N. Sanford, ed., *The American college.* John Wiley and Sons, 1962, 290-311.

Knox, W. D. A study of relationships of certain environmental factors to teaching success. *Journal of Experimental Education,* December 1956, 95-151.

Koen, F., & Ericksen. *An analysis of the specific features which characterize the more successful programs for the recruitment and training of college teachers.* Center for Research in Learning and Teaching, University of Michigan, 1967.

Kraybill, E. K. Effective teaching: institutes for engineering teachers. IEEE Transactions on *Education,* June 1969, 85-88.

Lazarsfeld, P. F., & Thielens, W. *The academic mind.* The Free Press, 1958.

Lee, C. B., ed. *Improving college teaching.* American Council on Education, 1967.

Luthans, F. *The faculty promotion process: an empirical analysis of the administration of large state universities.* Bureau of Business and Economics Research, University of Iowa, 1967.

McGee, R. *Academic janus.* Jossey-Bass, 1971.

McGrath, E. J. *The graduate school and the decline of liberal education.* Teachers College Press, Columbia University, 1959.

McGrath, E. J. *The predominantly Negro colleges in transition.* Teachers College Press, Columbia University, 1965.

McGrath, E. J., & Altman, I. *Small group research.* Holt, Rinehart and Winston, 1966.

McKeachie, W. J. Research on teaching at college and university level. In H. L. Gage, ed., *Handbook of Research on Teaching,* Rand McNally & Co., 1963, 1118-72.

Martin, W. B. *Conformity: standards and change in higher education.* Jossey-Bass, 1969.

Maslow, A. H. & Zimmerman, W. College teaching ability, scholarly ability, and personality. *Journal of Ed. Psychology,* 47:185-89, 1956.

Medsker, L. L. *The junior college.* McGraw-Hill, 1960.

Miller, W. S., & Wilson, K. M. *Faculty development procedures in small colleges/a southern survey.* Southern Regional Education Board, 1963.

Milton, O., & Shoben, E. J., Jr. *Learning and the professors.* Ohio University Press, 1968.

Monson, C. H., Jr. Teaching assistants: the forgotten faculty. *Educational Record.* Winter 1969, 60-65.

Mooney, W. T., Jr., & Brasted, R. C. *A report on the education and training of chemistry teachers for two-year colleges.* Advisory Council on College Chemistry, Stanford University, 1969.

Muscatine, C., ed. *Education at Berkeley.* Academic Senate, University of California at Berkeley, 1966.

Ness, F. *An uncertain glory.* Jossey-Bass, 1971.

Nichols, D., ed. *Perspectives on campus tensions.* American Council on Education, 1970.

Nowlis, V., Clark, K. E., & Rock, M. *The graduate student as teacher.* American Council on Education, 1968.

Pace, C. R. *College and university environment scales: Technical manual,* Princeton, New Jersey: Educational Testing Service, 1969.

Parsons, T., & Platt, G. M. *The American academic profession: A pilot study.* Laboratory of Social Relations, Harvard University, 1968.

Preparing two-year college teachers for the '70's. American Association of Junior Colleges, 1969.

Report of the president's commission on campus unrest (the Scranton report). *The Chronicle of Higher Education,* October 5, 1970.

Reusch, N. R. *The junior and community college faculty: a bibliography.* ERIC Clearinghouse for Junior College Information, 1969.

Rice, J. G. The campus climate: a reminder. In S. Baskin, ed. *Higher education: some newer developments.* McGraw-Hill, 1965, 304-317.

Riley, M. W., Foner, A., & associates. *Aging and society.* Vol. 1, An inventory of research findings, 1968.

Rogers, C. The facilitation of significant learning. In L. Siegel, ed. *Instruction: some contemporary viewpoints,* Chandler Publishing Co., 1967.

Rothwell, C. E., et. al. *The importance of teaching: a memorandum to the new college teacher.* The Hazen Foundation, 1968.

Runkel, P., Harrison, R., & Runkel, M., eds. *The changing college classroom.* Jossey-Bass, 1969.

Russell, J. D. Faculty satisfactions and dissatisfactions. *Journal of Experimental Education,* December 1962.

Sanford, N. *The American college.* Wiley, 1962.

_____. *Where colleges fail.* Jossey-Bass, 1967.

_____. whatever happened to action research? *Journal of Social Issues,* 26: 4, 1970.

Shugrue, M. The national study of English in the junior college. *Junior College Journal,* June-July, 1969.

Smith, P. Teaching, research, and publications as they affect academic performance and promotion. *Journal of Higher Education,* April 1961, 199-205.

Stecklein, J. E., & Lathrop, R. L. Faculty attraction and retention. *Bureau of Institutional Research,* University of Minnesota, 1960.

Stern, G. G. Characteristics of the intellectual climate in college environments. *Harvard Educational Review,* Winter 1963, 5-41.

Taylor, H. *Students without teachers: the crisis in the university.* McGraw-Hill, 1969.

The study of education at Stanford. Palo Alto, California: Stanford University, 1969.

Thornton, J. W., Jr., & Brown, J. W. *New media and college teaching.* National Education Association, 1968.

Tickton, S., ed. *To improve learning: an evaluation of instructional technology.* 2 vols., R. R. Bowker Co., 1970.

Trow, M., & Lipset, S. *National surveys of faculty and students in American higher education.* University of California at Berkeley, 1969.

Tussman, J. *Experiment at Berkeley.* Oxford University Press, 1969.

Vreeland, R. S., & Bidwell, C. E. Classifying university departments: an approach to the analysis of their effects upon undergraduates' values and attitudes. *Sociology of Education,* 1966, 237-254.

What they believe: a Fortune survey. *Fortune,* January 1969.

Whitehead, A. N. *Aims of education.* Macmillan, 1929.

Wilson, R. C., Gaff, J. G., & Bavry, J. L. *Manual of information for faculty characteristics questionnaire.* Center for Research and Development in Higher Education, University of California, Berkeley, 1970.

Woodburne, L. S. *Faculty personnel policies in higher education.* New York, 1950.

Wortham, M. The case for a doctor of arts degree: a view from junior college faculty. *AAUP Bulletin,* Winter 1967, 372-377.